The Long Road to Finding Me

The Long Road to Finding Me

The Childhood Years

By Lily Lane

©2026 Lily Lane

All rights reserved.

The author asserts her moral right to be identified as the author of this work.

This is a work of creative nonfiction. While based on the author's memories and experiences, some names, identifying details, and events have been changed, combined, or altered to protect the privacy of individuals. Any resemblance to actual persons, living or dead, is coincidental and not intended to harm or defame.

First Edition 2026

ISBN 978-1-9195159-0-8

Cover artwork by Niki Tang.

Dedication

For Nanny Clara,
who taught me that strawberries taste better when you steal them politely.

For James,
my first ever friend, who willingly sat next to me.

For Martin,
who let me down with his pinky promise.

For a boy,
who chased after Santa's trailer for sweets just for me.

For Denise,
the loyal friend who stuck around in all my chaos.

For the caretaker,
who cleaned up more of my experiments than anybody should have.

And for the dinner lady,
who fed me, spoiled me, and proved that kindness really did exist.

Acknowledgements

I would never have written this book without my family's support. To my husband, my son, and my daughter, thank you for believing in me when I did not believe in myself. Thank you for the gentle (and not-so-gentle) nudges, the pats on the back, and telling me I was doing well, even on days I thought I wasn't. Thank you for giving me permission to stop dedicating all my time to everyone else and allowing me to dedicate some of it to writing. To finally tell my story.

Your love is strong, and it made this book possible. I am truly thankful.

I love you guys, always.

Finally, my thanks to Niki for the cover artwork. This book would not feel the same without it.

Table of Contents

INTRODUCTION: THE BALANCE OF LIFE	1
ONE: VICKY'S FAMILY	5
TWO: FIRST MEMORIES	15
THREE: MEETING BABY SISTER	25
FOUR: SANTA'S FLOAT	39
FIVE: SURVIVAL CODE	47
SIX: FIRST DAY AT SCHOOL	53
SEVEN: CHRISTMAS	65
EIGHT: DAY TRIPS TO HOLIDAYS	71
NINE: LOCKED IN SCHOOL	79
TEN: TIED TO A CHAIR	85
ELEVEN: GIVING UP FOR LENT	91
TWELVE: BALLROOM DANCING	103

THIRTEEN: NEW FOREST HOLIDAYS	109
FOURTEEN: A PINKY PROMISE	115
FIFTEEN: ITCHING POWDER IN SCHOOL	123
SIXTEEN: READING A ROOM	131
SEVENTEEN: JUMPING OFF GARAGE ROOFS	137
EIGHTEEN: RUNNING OUT OF SCHOOL	147
NINETEEN: DOTTY	157
TWENTY: A LOST CHILD	167
TWENTY-ONE: DENISE, A TRUE FRIEND	173
TWENTY-TWO: JOHN'S WORLD	179
TWENTY-THREE: BRANDY THE GUARD DOG	187
TWENTY-FOUR: HORSE RIDING	197
TWENTY-FIVE: FLOODING SCHOOL	205
TWENTY-SIX: A PETITION	211

TWENTY-SEVEN: NANNY CLARA 213

TWENTY-EIGHT: STRANGER DANGER 221

Introduction: The Balance of Life

Before I Knew

Life, as I see it, is a balance.

A seesaw, like the ones you find in a playground, only this one is an emotional kind. It tips one way or the other, depending on how you feel.

Some people learn to sit somewhere around the middle. If the seesaw is steady, they feel steady. I never did.

From the very beginning, I lived at the extreme ends. Slammed down on one side, then launched into the air on the other.

Happiness, sadness, fear, safety. None of it ever came to me in small doses.

If something hurt, it crushed me.
If something felt good, it felt incredible.

There was no middle for me. No gentle sway. Only extremes.

Maybe you have felt that yourself, the kind where a tiny bit of kindness can light you up, and cruelty can shatter you.

When you live on the ends, everything hits so much harder.

I didn't understand any of this when I was younger.

Not the imbalance, not the whiplash of emotions, nor the way I was shaped by what happened to me.

I just knew highs and lows and clung to the highs for as long as possible.

Years later, I hit rock bottom. The seesaw crashed into the ground. It felt like it broke, and I couldn't balance it again.

I was so low, so exhausted, and one step away from giving up on myself. I didn't. I fought my way out, slowly and painfully. But I made it.

Writing was my therapy. Page by page, memory by memory, I began to understand how I had become who I was.

I needed to make sense of all the chaos, the extremes, the silence, the secrets, the hurt.

It was *The Long Road to Finding Me.*

I started writing this book when I was 47 years old, stopped, then picked it up at 57.

Some of the words came from a version of me who didn't yet understand everything. I was still under their influence.

The way I see the world now is nothing like how I saw it at 47. I see things differently. I have learnt things. I have let go of hate and learnt to forgive.

I understand so much more now, and that's why I had to finish my book.

So, as you read my story, I'm telling it through the eyes of a girl called Vicky. It helped me to write without pain and fall in love with her — myself.

Some parts of my story were told to me by my mother and grandmother. The rest is raw and honest but sometimes blurs at the edges.

It is my story, and how I escaped the trauma of my life. It's separated into five parts:

Childhood
Teens
Young adult
Married life
My thoughts now

That's what I hope for, as I'm still writing it.

Blimey! I think it is going to be an eye-opener for me too. I hope you enjoy it.

Now, let me take you to the beginning.

One: Vicky's Family

Vicky was born on a cold, crisp morning in March. Ann had been in pain all night. The contractions were strong and close together.

She struggled on silently throughout the night, trying not to wake her husband, John, who was sleeping deeply beside her.

It was around 6am. The pain was intense. Too much to bear. She had no choice but to wake John and ask him to ring for a midwife.

The phone box was twenty paces down the road. There were no mobile phones or a landline that we all take for granted today.

John shouted, "ALRIGHT, ALRIGHT, I HEAR YOU! Give me a minute to wake up!"

John was the one who liked to give orders, not take them. It didn't seem to matter to him that his precious daughter was about to be born.

He threw off the bed covers in a temper, shaved, got dressed, and made himself a cup of coffee as he did every morning.

Ann lay there in agony, listening to the scrape of his razor and the clink of his teaspoon, wishing he'd hurry up and call the midwife.

Maybe Ann would have liked a drink, a gentle back rub, even a few kind words. Better still, the bloody midwife. But no, she just had to wait.

As long as John was fine, that was all that mattered.

Ann was in labour with her second child, Vicky. So, let's pause for a moment to talk about her.

She didn't have an easy life. Too many siblings, not much stability, and never learnt how to stand her ground.

Vicky was born at home without any complications, except for a small tear. So, the very next day, John returned to work.

Ann was struggling. She was in pain from her stitches. She had a newborn who cried constantly, and she still had to look after their three-year-old daughter, Agnes.

She still had to clean, keep the house spotless, and have dinner ready by the time John walked through the door.

That was pretty normal back then, and she did it all without question.

Ann never asked him for help. She knew exactly how he'd react. If she ever did, John would make sure she knew he was doing her a huge favour.

When he came home from work, he would wander around the house looking for something out of place, just so he could complain. He was doing his best to wear her down.

Ann's life was hard. She accepted everything John threw at her, and she never challenged him. This was where the balance of her life finally tipped too far to one side.

Ann became very depressed. Everything revolved around John. Nothing good was happening in her life. Her spirit began to fade.

John, on the other hand, had all the control and power he wanted, but it wasn't enough. It didn't make him feel as good as it once did. He needed a lot more.

A few months after Vicky was born, Ann just couldn't take it anymore. She was hugely depressed and utterly exhausted.

Vicky cried constantly. She couldn't hold her milk down, even though she was ravenously hungry.

She would gulp it, then projectile vomit everywhere. Meanwhile, Agnes started demanding more and more attention from her mum.

She was being left to her own devices most of the time, and without Ann cleaning up behind her, her toys were everywhere.

But John didn't notice or care that Ann was crying out for help. Instead, he spent hours throwing sarcastic comments at her.

"Why is this place such a mess?" or "Hurry up, I'm hungry. Have you not washed up yet?"

John's favourite thing was to switch the television over, especially when Ann was watching it. He'd say, "Haven't you got better things to do?" He wore her down. She felt picked on.

Ann only found peace when John was at work. She felt free, even though she spent most of her time cleaning when she was able and preparing his dinner.

One afternoon, Ann finally snapped. Vicky was unwell, and Agnes was crying for attention. The pressure kept building inside Ann until she felt physically sick.

She had reached breaking point.

Rocking Vicky in her arms, with Agnes hanging off her apron, all Ann wanted to do was scream. She opened the bedroom window and held Vicky out of it.

For a moment, she thought it would be so easy to just let go, two storeys down, and the crying would stop.

She couldn't let go. She didn't want to let go. She just couldn't cope a minute longer.

Ann pulled Vicky back in and collapsed onto the floor, sobbing. She looked into her baby's eyes, then noticed Agnes, who was only three years old, staring at her.

Ann whispered, "I'm so sorry, I'm just tired and exhausted." Agnes said softly but quickly, "I can play with Vicky, Mummy. You go to sleep. I'm a big girl. I can look after her."

Ann gave her a feeble smile and went to lie down.

Life was very hard living with this man. John was extremely dominant and controlling.

As the years went on, he messed with Vicky's mind, forming pathways in her brain and shaping how she would see the world.

Nothing really changed. John started drinking, and at first it made him cheerful and affectionate. He even flirted with Ann in front of the children.

Every single night she went to bed with him and fulfilled his needs as usual. She had no choice.

John kept drinking, and Ann encouraged it. She thought it made him happy, and if he was happy, so was she.

Over the years, nobody noticed John becoming dependent on alcohol. He never drank to excess, but without it, his mood would change.

John drank whisky, sometimes four glasses a night, until it became a habit.

Ann made sure there was always whisky in the cupboard because without it, he became cruel, and she took the brunt of his moods.

It took her a long time to realise that withdrawal made him lash out.

If family came to visit, John seemed friendly and generous, offering everyone a drink so he wasn't drinking alone, and no one would suspect his dependence.

Every Thursday, John's cousin came around to watch television with the family. He was a very camp, gentle man who often babysat for them.

Agnes liked him a lot, but Vicky found his ways strange.

One evening when he came to visit, John encouraged his cousin, who wasn't a drinker, to have alcohol.

John found it hilarious when his cousin couldn't stand properly or fasten his coat as he was leaving.

Vicky was only little and heard the commotion. She climbed out of bed and peeked over the banister at the top of the stairs.

She didn't understand what she was seeing, only that something was wrong. For the first time, she saw someone extremely drunk, and it frightened her deeply.

Over time, John slipped into depression. The control over Ann didn't give him the same high as it once did.

John started to push boundaries, trying to find the fix that was now missing. As Vicky was growing up, he found it in her.

By letting his rudeness go unchecked, Ann was reinforcing his behaviour without even realising it.

Years later, Vicky would come to understand this differently. She came to resent both her parents, her father for what he did, and her mother for letting it continue.

At first, she felt deep sympathy for Ann. Her mother would talk endlessly about John's behaviour, pouring out her pain to Vicky.

But slowly, it became too much. A burden far too heavy for her to carry.

Eventually, Vicky learned to tune it out. She was tired of hearing Ann moan about John when she wouldn't leave him or tell him to stop.

Had she forgotten he was doing all this to Vicky too? That part was on her.

Vicky once asked her mum why she allowed John to treat them both so badly. Ann said, "I hate arguing. I had enough of it growing up with my own dad and siblings. I can't do it anymore."

Something shifted in Vicky. She knew she'd have to fight her own battles from now on. Her mum wasn't going to help.

But why did she argue with John in such a mean way if she hated arguing, especially as Vicky got older? It didn't make sense to her at all.

Two: First Memories

Vicky doesn't really have any memories from before she was four years old, except for three.

Her first memory was a day at nursery.

She didn't know where she was at the time. She only learned that years later when she was old enough to ask her mum.

Vicky remembered her mum handing her over at the door to a stranger. She clung tightly to her mum's hand, staring at the dark room she was about to be taken into.

It was a large square room that looked dark from the outside. A few children were crying, and an adult was telling them off. Nothing about it felt child-friendly at all.

These days, classrooms have bright pictures or children's work on the walls. This room had nothing. Just bare walls and a feeling that didn't belong anywhere near children.

A large, plump, cross-looking lady picked Vicky up and told her not to be silly. She prised her fingers from her mum's hand, and Ann left quickly.

Vicky cried while trying to escape the woman's arms, desperate to get back to her mother.

The woman held her in a tight grip, dragged her to a table, and forced her into a chair.

When Vicky tried to get up, she slapped her legs and snapped, "Look around at all the other children playing nicely. What do you think they think of you acting like this?"

Vicky went rigid and sank into that chair, her little heart pounding, a thousand eyes staring. She was handed puzzle pieces and told to stay there until she was told otherwise.

She still remembers the fear to this day, but nothing else, not even her mum coming to release her. For reasons she never understood, she never went back.

Her second memory was visiting an older lady who always seemed pleased to see her.

Vicky would sit on the floor and play with whatever toys were brought out for her, while Ann and this lady chatted for most of the morning.

These tea-and-chat mornings happened about once a week. Vicky didn't mind because the lady was very nice.

Years later, when Vicky was an adult, she asked her mum about those visits. She was already half-guessing the truth.

Ann told her the lady had been the mother of her first husband. They met in secret, mostly when John was at work, because he didn't want Ann to have any contact with her.

Ann seemed quite surprised that Vicky remembered those visits at all. She asked her not to say anything, even after all those years.

Ann had assumed she was far too young to remember, but clearly, she wasn't.

Her third memory was a happier one: playing under a huge kitchen table, beside a bay window, and next to some kitchen units.

She had to strain her neck to look up, always wondering what sat on that high sideunit above her. A navy-blue and white radio played in the background.

Ann listened to *Woman's Hour* while she ironed, and Vicky listened to *Listen with Mother*. Vicky loved that radio. She always tried to reach the knobs.

She was fascinated by the white noise that crackled out when she twiddled with them.

Sometimes, when Ann was ironing, she let Vicky turn the kitchen table upside down and cover it with a sheet to make a den.

Vicky had a huge teddy that she loved dearly, called Ted. He was the only male in her life she trusted.

She told him all her worries, cuddled him when she'd been in trouble, and tried to carry him everywhere.

When she was having a fun time playing, Ted had to be in the thick of it. He was always with her. Bump, bump, bump as she dragged him down the stairs behind her.

Ann had sewn up his nose about five times. That poor bear had been in the toy hospital more times than Vicky could remember.

She loved to dress him in her old, clean (I might add) pants and a knitted tank top her mum had made, now far too small for her to wear.

Vicky didn't get much alone time with her mum. Her older sister, Agnes, was very jealous and pushed her out at every opportunity.

So, when Agnes was at school, those moments with her mum felt precious. Vicky loved to play bus conductors on the stairs. The games were always short, leaving her disappointed each time.

Her mum tried to start a game to spark Vicky's imagination and then slip away, but it never worked. She desperately wanted her mum to stay and play with her.

Ann would say, "I can't play. I've got so much work to do." But that often meant sitting for hours doing crossword puzzles, sinking deeper into her depression.

As Vicky got a little older and learned to play by herself, her imagination took over. She could empty her toy cupboard in a matter of minutes.

She held tea parties, played board games with imaginary friends, and ran her own school with crayons, paper, and her dolls. If she could imagine it, Vicky could play it.

Ann would often call out, "Quick, quick! Let's tidy up. Daddy will be home soon. If he sees this mess, he'll be so mad."

Vicky always tidied fast. She was so scared of him that she did it with haste. Intentionally or not, Ann was teaching her to fear her father.

The rest of Vicky's very early memories under the age of four have faded.

Snoopy, her cat, the birth of her sister, Christmas, playing on the streets, and starting school are the next strongest. So, this is where I want to begin.

Vicky had a cat named Snoopy, a jet-black cat she adored. He spent most of his time at the neighbour's house, but whenever he was around, Vicky spent most of her time with him.

Snoopy gave her the attention nobody else did, a stand-in parent, in a way.

Vicky tried to stay clear of her father. He was cross a lot of the time, her sister was mean, and her mother had no time for her, now she was at school.

Snoopy gave her the comfort and love she needed.

When Vicky was six, Snoopy came into the house with blood dripping from his mouth. She overheard that he had either been kicked or hit by a car.

The neighbour had taken him to the vets a couple of times to try to help him. Ann didn't drive, so she couldn't take him herself, and Vicky's dad, well, no one ever said why he wasn't involved.

Vicky remembered the last time she saw her cat. It was heartbreaking.

It was a school morning. She ran into the living room to check on Snoopy. He was lying on crumpled newspaper on the sofa.

She stroked his fur as gently as possible, feeling his pain and wishing she could take his discomfort away.

Snoopy sat up and stretched, blood and dribble running from his mouth. He nudged Vicky's hand aside so he could climb weakly onto her lap.

She knew her lap was small, but she tried to make herself as big and comfortable as possible.

Vicky refused breakfast and ignored the urge to use the toilet because she didn't want to disturb her poor little injured baby.

She whispered to Snoopy that she would buy him one of those brown fur rugs to snuggle up on. It would be much more comfortable than that tatty newspaper.

On Sunday, she would save up all her school sweet money to buy him one.

It wasn't long before the neighbour turned up with a brown wicker cage. Ann always seemed jumpy when someone came to the door.

Visitors made her stiffen for reasons Vicky didn't understand.

Ann quickly asked Vicky to place Snoopy in the cage because he was off to the vets again.

She did it quickly, because he hated going in there, meowing loudly and looking at her with those big green eyes that always made her feel guilty.

As the neighbour turned to leave, she asked Vicky if she wanted to say goodbye for the last time.

"Last time? Why is it the last time?" Vicky asked.

Ann quickly ushered her away from the front door, not wanting her to make a scene, and said, "Because he's off to heaven and won't be coming back."

Then she closed the door quickly on the neighbour. Vicky started to cry, certain she had helped him die by putting him in that basket.

She thought Snoopy would blame her. If only she could have helped him escape instead.

She got herself in a right old state. She didn't understand or accept what was happening and ran off to her bedroom, too heartbroken to move.

Ann was frustrated. She had to get Agnes and Vicky to school, but Vicky was making them late by refusing to go.

"Pull yourself together! You're being really stupid. It's just a damn cat," Ann shouted in an extremely loud, cross voice.

She grabbed Vicky by the shoulder, turned her around, smacked her across the bottom, and pushed her out of the bedroom door.

Vicky retreated into herself. She hated the world. She had to mourn and forget, all by herself.

Three: Meeting Baby Sister

When Vicky was five, she remembered the day her little sister Gwen was born. At the time, she and Agnes had scarlet fever.

Vicky wasn't as ill as Agnes, and in those days, being unwell meant confinement to bed.

Ann gave birth to Gwen at home. As labour pains intensified, so did the noise. Vicky and Agnes, who had been confined to bed, were sent downstairs so they didn't have to listen.

They sat with John and found it happily strange, if there is such a phrase, to be eating breakfast with him. A breakfast that he had actually prepared.

Vicky felt as proud as punch that her dad had actually done something for her, even if it was only cornflakes.

For once, John talked to his children, and Vicky could feel herself letting her guard down.

She could see this clueless, gentle man, out of his depth, trying to make small talk with his daughters.

Every few minutes John ran upstairs, and when he came back down, he said, "Not yet." After a while, they stopped asking if the baby was born. It felt like it was taking forever.

Vicky told her dad she would look after the baby every day for Mummy and that they should call her Sarah.

John said, "What if it's a boy?" But Vicky knew for sure it wouldn't be a boy. The thought hadn't even crossed her mind.

Gwen came into the world without any problems. Vicky and Agnes were allowed a quick peek at her once she was all cleaned up and sleeping.

Vicky felt an instant bond. At the time, she didn't realise how much of an impact this tiny bundle would have on her life.

A few days later, Vicky was well enough to get out of bed and help the midwife bathe the baby.

Vicky felt such warmth towards the midwife. She had given her a rare happy moment, making her feel important as she passed the soap and powder.

When they had finished, Vicky gave the midwife a big hug. Ann's face tightened the moment she saw it.

Something in her expression made Vicky tense up. She recognised that look immediately. Ann rushed forward and said, "Back to bed now, come on."

Not wanting to go, Vicky whined, "I want to dress Gwen, pleeeeeease? And I can help feed her; I can rock her to sleep too."

The midwife smiled and said, "I can see you are going to be a fantastic big sister. You need to help your mum as much as possible, because it's demanding work bringing up a baby."

Vicky had the biggest grin on her face she could manage, until Ann grabbed her by the arm so roughly that it hurt.

Ann mouthed, "Bed! Now!" The midwife was still focused on the baby and didn't notice.

Vicky's heart sank. She didn't know what she had done wrong, but it must have been something. She slipped off to her bedroom without another word.

As the midwife was leaving, she popped her head into Vicky's room to say goodbye. Ann was standing behind her, scowling.

Vicky recognised that look instantly, so she smiled sweetly and stayed silent.

"I reckon you could get up today," the midwife said. "I can't see that rash anymore. She's fine to touch the baby. Remember what I said. Help your mum. That's a good girl."

Then she turned to Agnes. "Oh, you poor girl. I'm afraid it's a few more days in bed for you," she added softly.

As Ann walked the midwife to the door, Agnes stuck her tongue out at Vicky, snatched a doll from her hands, and shouted, "Get off my bed!"

Vicky, only five years old, could still land a punch. Agnes immediately wailed, loudly enough to make sure their mum could hear.

It always went the same way, Agnes pushed, Vicky reacted, and Vicky was the one who was punished.

Ann stormed up the stairs, livid, probably because the midwife was still on the doorstep and heard the commotion.

Agnes, of course, took immense pleasure in telling her mum that Vicky had hit her, conveniently leaving out why.

Vicky tried to defend herself, but her mum wasn't listening. Ann grabbed her off the bed and smacked her three times across the bottom.

Vicky glanced over at Agnes, who was grinning. It only made her even angrier.

She lay on her bed, not talking to anyone, already plotting how she was going to make Agnes pay.

A few weeks later, Vicky woke up and was excited to help her mum. It was a Saturday. An entire day with her baby sister. She dressed so fast that her jumper was inside out.

"Mum, is Gwen awake? Can I dress her?" Vicky shouted as she ran into her parents' bedroom.

There was a scramble under the bedclothes. John popped his head out, looking flushed and furious.

"Get out, you stupid girl! Get out!"

Vicky froze for a second. The air had gone from her chest. She wondered what she had done wrong.

Her father threw his slipper at her, hitting her full force in the face. Heartbroken, she didn't dare cry.

Frozen for a split second from the shock, she shrank inside herself. She knew she had to get out of there quickly.

With her head down, she retreated to her room, only to be mocked by Agnes the moment she walked in.

Vicky had no personal space. Wherever she went or whatever she did, someone was there being mean to her.

Vicky and Agnes were called down for breakfast. Vicky stood at the bottom of the stairs holding her breath, hoping the day was going to get better.

As she entered the kitchen, Ann was bottle-feeding Gwen and John was sorting out breakfast. Vicky started to approach her mum and the baby, but her dad cut her off.

"Get to the table, leave your mother alone. You've given us enough grief this morning. It's all about you, isn't it?"

He slammed a bowl of porridge down in front of Vicky and gently placed one down in front of Agnes, then ruffled her hair.

All Vicky could do was look at them with scorn, even though what she really wanted to do was run away.

Agnes loved porridge, but the thick slime made Vicky gag. Tears rolled down her cheeks. She couldn't hold them in any longer.

"Eat your bloody breakfast! I've had as much as I can take from you, you ungrateful little girl!" John shouted.

Ann stood up to burp the baby. John turned his back and began washing the dishes, banging them loudly to make his point without speaking a word.

He hated housework. He believed it was women's work.

Agnes finished her breakfast and spat her last mouthful into Vicky's bowl. Vicky's cries intensified. She didn't speak in case it made things worse.

Her father dropped a plate, and the crash set him off. He grabbed Vicky by the hair. Furious, he dragged her out of the kitchen.

Vicky sat shaking on the stairs, wondering what she had done wrong. When everybody had finished eating, he called her back in.

John spoke aggressively through gritted teeth, "You're such a spoiled brat. You're the cause of all the arguments in this house."

He was at boiling point now. "Why can't you ever be happy? Your mum and I are arguing, and that's your fault."

"Sit back down and eat your porridge. It's cold now." He placed the bowl back in front of her.

"Agnes and your mum are going up to bathe the baby, and I don't want to hear another word out of your mouth. Eat. Now get on with it."

Vicky stared at the patch where Agnes had spat into her bowl. She tried to mash it into the porridge, hoping to hide it, but the thought wouldn't leave her head.

She tried to explain what Agnes had done, but before the words even came out, John grabbed her by the arm and smacked her repeatedly until he felt better.

"Don't try to blame other people," he barked. "It won't wash with me. Your sister is nothing but nice to you, you little cow!"

Vicky folded and sat quietly at the table for what felt like hours. At least she was out of everyone's way.

She listened to the giggles upstairs and the cooing over the baby.

John had gone into the sitting room to read the newspaper. He needed the silence to read, so in a way, she was safer in the kitchen.

Vicky had become everybody's emotional and physical punching bag.

Feeling guilty, Ann came quietly downstairs. She picked up Vicky's breakfast bowl and emptied the contents straight into the bin.

"No, Mummy, no! Daddy said I have to eat it. I'm going to be in more trouble now," Vicky said, trembling.

Ann looked at her with guilt written across her face and said, "Don't worry, darling. Stay out of your father's way. He'll forget all about it later. When Gwen wakes up, if you behave, you can go and play with her."

Vicky climbed the stairs. With Agnes out in the garden, she finally had the bedroom to herself.

She started to grin and placed a few bogies under her sister's pillow. "Gotcha!" she thought.

Later that day, John found the porridge in the bin. Ann owned up to throwing it away. Vicky could hear them arguing downstairs.

"You say I do nothing in this house," John shouted, "but when I try, you undermine me! You tell me Vicky needs discipline, then you say I'm too harsh! What do you want from me?"

"You're good for nothing," Ann snapped back. "I want a divorce. God knows why I married you, you're useless!" She couldn't have made him feel any smaller if she tried.

The arguing was relentless.

Vicky sat with her hands over her ears, hoping it would stop.

She thought about how to do better, how she could get them to see she was a nice person and that she was someone who just wanted to feel loved by them, not hated.

It wasn't long before John entered Vicky's room, smelling of booze.

His voice was mellow, but his words still stung. He told Vicky he hoped she was happy now, that she caused it all.

Vicky stared at her blanket, not saying a word, hoping it would protect her. He went back downstairs to watch the television, and the house fell silent for the rest of the day.

She stayed in her room. She'd lost interest in playing with the baby. It felt pointless now. She lay there, deep in thought, trying to work out how she could be better.

More than anything, she had wanted to be able to play with her older sister and tell her everything. Now all hopes were on her little sister. She just wished Gwen would grow up a little quicker.

Years later, Vicky found out from her mother that John hadn't really wanted children.

He only warmed to the idea if it meant having a son, so when his first child was a girl, it was a big disappointment to him.

They tried again and Vicky arrived, another girl. She was born on the same date Ann's first husband had died, but eight years later. Her birthday became a gentle reminder.

Then, their third child was born on the same date Ann's late husband was buried, but thirteen years later. Another girl, another blow, another reminder.

To add to his misery, John had wanted a boy, and it wasn't in his control.

Vicky always sensed a little tension around her birthday. It had something to do with Ann's past. So, let's dive into that.

Ann's childhood wasn't easy. She grew up in a very large family, one of seven sisters, three older and three younger.

There was constant fighting and arguing, mostly over clothes. If you had nothing to wear, you simply stole from your sisters.

She spent parts of her childhood in and out of children's homes because her mum and dad kept losing their house to debt. They struggled to feed and clothe their children.

Debt collectors often turned up at the house and the kids were left to answer the door. They had to lie and say their parents weren't home.

They just couldn't keep up with payments. It didn't help that her father was a gambler.

Two of Ann's sisters were adopted out because the family couldn't afford to keep them.

Ann should have been adopted too, but her mother changed her mind when she saw how distressed Ann became.

For a bit of a deeper dive, Ann's mother Clara, was adopted herself. She also had a hard life.

Her birth mother was just eighteen and pregnant by a soldier, and simply not ready to keep her.

Clara grew up near where her biological mother lived but rarely saw her. Her adoptive parents were very unkind.

Maybe understanding Clara's pain was why Vicky loved her nan so much.

The past never really goes away. It finds its own way of being passed down.

Now Clara, Ann's mother, also had a sister, who was adopted into a different home. They stayed in contact, but her sister's life took a darker turn.

Desperate for money, she became a prostitute. Her husband had encouraged it because he liked the money it brought in.

She even tried to pull Clara into that life. But Clara refused and tried to talk her out of it.

Her sister had married at sixteen. She was still incredibly young. At eighteen she was raped, strangled, and murdered.

Her body was found in a wasteland with abrasions from the fight she put up as she tried to escape.

Clara took it hard. Her sister had been the only real family she had left.

Pain had travelled through the women in this family long before Vicky was even born.

As Ann grew older, she became desperate to leave home. She met a man old enough to be her father and married him at seventeen.

The marriage didn't last long. One day in March, he woke up early in the morning, unable to breathe, and died suddenly from an asthma attack. The grief shattered her.

Ann moved back home. Unhappy, she rushed into a second marriage, this time with John.

Ann's family didn't like him at all. They found him arrogant and disrespectful. Either Ann couldn't see it, or she chose to ignore it. From my experience, it would have been the latter.

Now you can see why Vicky sensed tension on her birthday. If Vicky's birthday fell on a weekend, the family would visit Ann's late husband's grave.

They would tidy it up or repaint the letters on his headstone.

Vicky didn't mind this too much because next to the graveyard, there was a forest walk that she loved to explore. Most of her time was spent playing on the streets.

Vicky was born into chaos. With Gwen's arrival, it only got worse.

Four: Santa's Float

It wasn't long after Gwen was born that Vicky formed a strong bond with her sister. She spent most of her time playing with her sister in the playpen.

Ann used this to her advantage. She would say, "You're such a good big sister. Gwen loves you so much."

This made Vicky smile. Somebody loving her was huge. "You are so helpful, looking after Gwen for me," Ann would add. Vicky beamed from ear to ear.

Most days, Ann heard, "Mummy, can you lift me into the playpen? I need to look after Gwen. I think she wants me to play."

Ann was happy to oblige; it meant less childcare for her. Her sweet-talking had worked.

The only problem was that after about an hour or so, Vicky would get bored and want to go and do her own thing. Ann would use guilt to keep her there.

She started off being nice, saying, "Gwen will be sad if you go. She loves you so much and really loves the games you play."

It worked for a bit, tugging on Vicky's pure, kind heart.

When Vicky started to whine because she'd really had enough, that's when Ann's tone changed and the nastiness would come out.

"Oh, you're so selfish! She needs you. Why do you get her so excited if you don't want to play?"

Vicky knew exactly how that felt, so sometimes she stayed, determined to prove that she wasn't selfish and was, actually, a really nice girl.

When Gwen was allowed to play on the floor, Vicky grew anxious. She couldn't relax if Gwen went anywhere near the hallway.

Part of that fear came from her own past. She had trauma from falling down the stairs repeatedly as a toddler.

She was small, but she remembered it like it was yesterday. Another memory that stayed with her into her adult life.

Ann would take Agnes upstairs and sit her on a stool in front of the big bedroom mirror, plaiting or gathering her hair into a ponytail, getting her ready for school.

She left Vicky downstairs alone with no toys. Those stayed upstairs unless it was Christmas.

Vicky didn't like to be separated. She felt scared.

She would climb the stairs on her hands and knees and as she reached the top, she would stand up, lose her balance, and tumble back down.

Eventually, a pram was put at the bottom of the stairs to block her way.

Vicky could see the wheels with their white rubber tyres. They were very large, with a small gap between the front and rear wheel that she could squeeze through.

Falling down the stairs hurt even more now, crashing into the back of that pram. Vicky never stopped climbing — she never learnt.

All she wanted was not to be alone and to be a princess, sitting on a throne in front of her mother's mirror while having her hair done.

Vicky had curly, messy hair, and Ann preferred to keep it short if she had the time to cut it. Vicky didn't realise her hair was short, not really. She believed it was long and shiny like Rapunzel's.

She hadn't really seen herself in a mirror, something her mother kept her away from.

The memory of falling on the stairs stayed with her for years. Now that Gwen was here, Vicky worried she might try to climb the stairs and fall too.

Whenever Gwen was crawling, Vicky followed her everywhere, keeping her safe.

There were photos of Vicky throughout the toddler years. In nearly all of them, she had big bruises on her forehead. Almost certainly from the stairs.

Around the same time, one Christmas Eve, John allowed Agnes and Vicky to stand at the front gate and watch Santa's float go past.

A boy, not much older than Agnes, asked, "Do you like sweets? I can get some from the trailer if you like?"

"Yes, please!" Vicky replied eagerly. Moments like this meant the world to her.

Nobody ever did anything nice for her, so even the smallest acts of kindness felt magical. Two ends of the balancing scale.

The boy ran off to fetch a few sweets from the trailer. Agnes looked most displeased, mainly because she had been ignored.

John had come to the front door to watch the float. He noticed Vicky had her nightie on back to front and inside out again.

Nobody helped her get dressed. She had learned all by herself and was proud of it.

John looked at Vicky and took in how she was dressed. His face changed instantly.

Through gritted teeth, he said, "Get inside! Your nightie is inside out. People will think we don't dress you properly. Get inside now!"

Vicky told her father that a boy was fetching sweets for her. She wanted to wait for him so she could say thank you.

She knew it was rude to just walk away. At the time, she was thinking more about the boy than the sweets themselves.

But that only seemed to make John even angrier. "I said inside now, unless you want a bloody good hiding, right here and now!"

Vicky replied, "But Santa hasn't passed properly yet." John stamped on her toes, hard.

Vicky held in the noise she needed to make from the pain, then hobbled inside to fix her nightie.

As she ran back to the front door, her father slammed it shut. "He's gone now," he said crossly. "He told me that if you don't buck your ideas up, there will be no presents for you this year."

Agnes giggled. John handed her some of the sweets the boy had fetched.

"They're mine!" Vicky protested. John unwrapped one and popped it slowly into his mouth. "Hope you choke," Vicky thought to herself.

Wherever he is now, thank you to that boy who showed Vicky some kindness on Christmas Eve back in the seventies. It stayed with her for years, that she never got to say thank you personally.

To Vicky it was such a big deal. Kindness towards her was a rarity, so when it happened it felt amazing. A small act of kindness could go such a long way.

Ann very rarely stuck up for Vicky, but this time she had seen what John had done with the sweets.

When nobody was around, she quietly opened a tin of Quality Street, peeling the sticky tape very carefully so she could reseal it later without anyone knowing.

"Take one of these," she whispered. "Give me the wrapper so I can hide it from your father." It was such a little gesture, but it made Vicky feel seen and comforted.

Another early memory from that time, just before Vicky started school, was how much freedom she had outside before Gwen was born.

Vicky was four years old, playing out on the streets, and she loved it. She felt free.

Ann trusted her to go to the corner shop by herself, even before she had started school.

The first time, her mum gave her a pound note and told her to buy some bread and milk.

Vicky skipped off singing, "Bread and milk! Bread and milk!" She knew the way. She had been with her mother countless times.

There was one small road to cross that was never busy. Ann often got Vicky to cross them both over the road when they went to the shops together. Vicky felt safe to do it by herself.

Inside the shop, she had a good look around, thinking she could take her time.

Then, she realised her mum was probably waiting for the shopping.

She quickly grabbed baked beans, paid for them, waited for her change (well, the cashier called her back for her change) and then ran all the way home.

Ann thought it was very funny that bread and milk turned into baked beans.

Five: Survival Code

Vicky had two friends: Nina, her next-door neighbour, and Tracy, who lived a few doors up, next to Mrs Hemlock, the cat lady.

Mrs Hemlock's house always looked a bit eerie to Vicky.

The front door was dark green, making the house look very dim inside. There was a strong smell of cat urine that hit you the moment you walked past.

Mrs Hemlock was tall, thin, and incredibly old. The children on the street believed she was a witch and someone to fear.

In Vicky's mind, she had killed Snoopy, her cat. No doubt his innards were in some kind of spell potion. She loved telling the street kids exactly what the cat lady had done.

Mrs Hemlock had a grown-up son too. He was tall and lanky, older than Vicky's parents, with long, untidy black hair, and he walked with a limp.

Vicky decided he was Frankenstein, stitched together from body parts his mother had collected.

All the parents on the street warned their kids to stay away from that house.

When Vicky called on her friend Tracy, she stayed on high alert in case either of them came out of their house.

Tracy lived next door to the cat lady. Vicky would hold her breath until she turned blue, bouncing up and down on the doorstep while waiting for her friend to answer.

Ann encouraged Vicky to play outside, mostly to keep her out of John's firing line. With a new baby and John's constant temper, Ann was struggling to keep the house together.

Having Vicky out from under her feet made life easier.

Agnes was around seven or eight, old enough to help with simple chores, which pushed four- or five-year-old Vicky further aside.

Once Gwen was born, Ann focused completely on the baby. Vicky was left with the scraps, the verbal digs, the physical blows, and the rejection from her mum, dad, and older sister.

Vicky was starting to develop a tough outer shell. From a very young age, she learned not to trust people.

She defended herself as best she could and began forming her own ideas that no one supported.

Parents should help their children explore ideas safely. Vicky's parents quashed any idea she had or used it as ammunition against her.

Everybody knows the saying about dangling a carrot in front of a donkey. It follows and does as you ask, as long as the carrot stays in sight.

John and Ann treated Vicky and her emotions a bit like that. They dangled things and promises that lit her up, only to snatch them away as she got too close.

For John, it was power. For Vicky, it was damage. The kind that shapes who you become.

John, Agnes, and even Ann at times found ways to belittle her. Games always ended with Vicky crying and running away, only for someone to say, "Don't take everything to heart, you always spoil the fun, it always has to be about you."

It was never about the game. They just enjoyed making her small.

One particular walk with the family, stayed with her. John had been playfully poking her and she poked back. He picked her up, swung her, then put her on the floor.

John never played. It was totally out of character. Vicky didn't care; she was loving his attention.

Then, without warning, he stopped. No signal. No explanation.

Vicky kept poking, hoping he would pick her up. Instead, John stopped walking and out of nowhere said, "You just don't know when to stop, do you?"

Two seconds ago, she had been so happy. Now his voice stripped everything away.

"Have we not taught you anything? People can't always do what you want. Yet again, it's all about you. Just stop."

Vicky waited for the ground to swallow her. For the rest of that walk, she held in her tears. She wasn't allowed to cry.

Every now and again, Agnes clipped her ankles and grinned. Vicky was paralysed. She couldn't fight back.

Playing with friends was Vicky's escape. Even then, she didn't always understand the rules.

She preferred her own games, the only place where nobody could twist things, cheat, or hurt her.

She didn't realise her friends weren't like her parents. She had been trained to expect unfair play.

So, she built her own survival code:

Don't share anything unless you're ready to lose it.
Don't let anyone else lead the game.
Be the strongest.
Control or be controlled.

Vicky had no idea people could be kind. She knew nothing about friendships.

If somebody liked what she liked, they were friends. If they didn't, they were the enemy and pushing them around might make them cooperate.

It never worked the way she hoped, and it certainly didn't help when she started school.

Through all of this, she was desperate for Agnes to be her friend.

She tried to please her in every way, hoping for affection. But Vicky was naive. Agnes simply enjoyed getting her into trouble.

Six: First Day at School

It was Vicky's first day at school. Agnes had left early to meet her friends. Ann hated the school run at the best of times, but it was Vicky's first day, so she had no choice but to take her in.

Vicky had been given some pocket money by her nan, so she stopped at the corner shop on the way.

She bought herself a packet of crisps and some rainbow sherbet. If school meant she got to spend ten pence every morning, this whole school business might actually be fun.

As she got closer to the school, she could hear the roar of children playing. Her whole body started to tremble. She didn't like crowds, noise, or the feeling of being watched.

Ann bent down to Vicky, seeing how stressed she was, and whispered, "Do not make a scene. You must not cry, do you hear me?"

Vicky nodded, sucking in a deep breath. She didn't want to let her mum down.

She watched the children play in silence, knowing she was going to be joining them very soon.

The whistle blew and the children lined up. Vicky spotted Agnes and waved.

Agnes stuck her tongue out and made a gesture that basically meant, "I don't know you, stay away."

After the older children went inside, a friendly teacher spoke to all the new ones waiting at the gates.

She asked them to enter the playground, then greeted everybody. It was time for parents and children to follow her into school.

She led them through the main doors. PE bags hung from hooks and the strong smell of cheesy feet drifted over them.

Next was a room with no doors. It had about six sinks on each side and one drinking fountain, which was pointed out to them on the way.

They went through a set of heavy double doors and out to another area. The teacher said, "This is your playground for your first four years."

She told the parents that children up to year four were out in the prefab buildings.

The tall chimneys on the roof of the main school were unstable, so they had closed the upper floor of the school until they had the money to rectify the problem.

Vicky realised she wouldn't be mixing with her older sister. She wasn't sure if this was a bad thing or not.

She was taken into the first classroom. Children were already seated.

Vicky spotted Nina, sitting at a large table surrounded by friends. She waved enthusiastically but Nina scowled and looked away.

The teacher noticed, smiled, and said, "Oh, don't worry, you'll make lots of friends here. Come with me. I've got a special table with some things on it just for you."

Vicky followed eagerly without a backward glance, curious about what she'd get.

Once all of the children were seated, the teacher started to talk.

"Hi, my name is Miss Morgan, and I am your teacher for this year." She had such a bubbly voice.

"I want the rest of the children to welcome the new arrivals." She then went over to speak to Nina.

When Vicky looked up, her mum had already gone. She felt sad because she didn't get to wave goodbye.

Vicky looked around. She had two girls on her table. One was crying silently, the other had her arms folded with a face like thunder.

She looked over to Nina for reassurance but saw Nina getting a stern telling-off from Miss Morgan. She was also pointing in Vicky's direction.

When Miss Morgan walked back to her desk, Nina screwed up her face at Vicky.

The sting of rejection hit immediately. Vicky felt tears rising but remembered what her mum had said to her.

Now, because Vicky was born in March, she didn't start school until the Easter term.

Nina, born in November, started at the beginning of term in September. A full six months before Vicky, and she had her own circle of friends. She didn't want Vicky joining them.

Vicky remembered her first day of school so clearly. She was given a pencil, a rubber, a pencil case, two notebooks, a drawer, and something magical: a sentence maker. A big, stiff card folder filled with loose keywords she could pull out to build sentences with.

Miss Morgan spoke to the class and sent them to their designated areas.

"Children on this table, you are reading. Your table, you're painting," she said, pointing as she went. "At your table you can play with sand and water and dress up."

Vicky sat there worried, wondering what she was going to be asked to do.

"The new children, go pick up a square piece of carpet and sit in front of the blackboard over there."

There were lots of squeaky chairs and chatter until everybody was where they should be. Vicky stayed frozen to her chair.

Miss Morgan came over gently. "What's your favourite colour?" "Green," Vicky whispered.

The teacher found Vicky a piece of carpet in that colour, took her hand, placed the carpet next to her chair, and asked her to sit down.

Then came the first task.

"In a minute, I want you all to go back to your seats quietly. Place your rubber and pencil in your case, and place everything in your drawer except your sentence maker.

Then take your drawer and place it in the unit over there. Then, come back and sit down on your mat." The teacher spoke clearly and calmly.

Vicky began to cry as all the children started to get up. There were a lot of instructions in such a busy room.

A boy next to her, calm and kind, put his arm around her. "I'll help you," he said softly. "Where is your table?" Vicky pointed.

He held her hand and helped her, then she helped him. He even moved someone else's tray so he could be next to hers.

Vicky started to smile. She had just made her first friend. His name was James.

Miss Morgan explained how the sentence maker worked. For the rest of the task, they were left to see what they could do with it.

Vicky knew how to write her name and realised it was printed as a keyword. She picked it up and went over to show James. They both presented it proudly to Miss Morgan.

Vicky earned a star, one for her jumper, one on the wall chart. This started a chain reaction. Everybody started to look for their names.

After a little while, each table rotated. Vicky was sent to a playhouse with dressing-up clothes. Everybody was pushing and shoving, so Vicky just walked around with James, looking at everything.

At about eleven o'clock, milk bottles with a straw were given out to everybody. It was the best-tasting milk Vicky had ever tried. It was so creamy.

There were four bottles left. Miss Morgan said, "Four children who work the hardest can drink the rest of the milk if they want it. At the end of the day, mind." Vicky could see her name on a bottle.

Playtime arrived. Vicky went outside and approached Nina and her friends. "Can I play?" Vicky asked softly. "No," Nina snapped. "There's no character left for you."

Vicky tried other girls in the group, but she got the same reaction and was told to go away.

She found a corner where two buildings met, faced the wall so she couldn't see the children, and stood there alone until the whistle blew.

Glad to be inside, she was given sand and water to play with. James joined her and they had a lot of fun.

At lunchtime, Ann waited outside the door. Vicky kept waving. Her mum gestured for her to stop.

When she arrived home, Ann had moved a table in front of the television. Vicky ate her lunch while watching *Rainbow*. After she finished, she headed upstairs, but Ann was quick to call her back.

"Drink up. I need to get you back to school."

"Again?" Vicky asked. She thought the day was over. "Oh no."

That afternoon wasn't so bad. She got to draw squiggle lines in her books and paint. School always finished with a story and some singing.

Vicky and James were offered the extra milk. Vicky was chuffed and couldn't wait to tell her mum.

From the first day, Vicky got along better with boys.

She was quite a pretty child. She was skinny and had blonde curly hair. The boys adored her. Vicky loved the attention the boys gave her, something her family couldn't. She needed affection so badly she clung to every scrap of it.

James became her first boyfriend, though they were only little.

He had special needs, likely ADHD or autism, though no one really used those words back then in the seventies.

Vicky was gentle with him. He adored her.

They held hands constantly. He once walked up to a dinner lady and announced, "This is my girlfriend. Look, we even kiss!" And planted a quick peck on Vicky's lips.

But James struggled. One day, overwhelmed, he grabbed a metre ruler that was as thick as a plank of wood and began swinging it wildly in class.

He often had violent outbursts that were a cause for concern. Miss Morgan chased him around the classroom, shouting for help from another class next door.

Vicky managed to take the ruler from him. James was removed from class. Vicky was terribly upset. She could hear James wailing and sounding distressed from the other room.

The headmistress called Vicky aside. "James could use a friend right now," she said softly. Vicky didn't hesitate. She sat with him, hugged him, and talked to him until he calmed down enough to return to class.

A couple of days later, Vicky and another boy were called into the corridor. They were both told that James wouldn't be coming back to school after he'd been missing for a few days.

"He is going to a special school to help with his bad moods," Miss Morgan said.

"I'm in a bad mood, so can I go with him?" Vicky asked.

The teacher smiled sadly. "Unfortunately, you can't, but James would love to get a letter from you both. If I help you to write it, would you be up for it?"

She was eager and wrote one immediately. She couldn't wait for his reply, but it never came.

Vicky had become really close to him. He was her only friend and now he had been taken away.

The one good thing was that Vicky was collecting a lot of stars for her chart, beating everybody by miles. She was very proud of herself.

But socially, she struggled. Especially with girls. She preferred one special friend over a whole group.

Put her in a crowd and she froze.

She worried constantly about what people thought of her, convinced she wasn't valued, just like at home.

Over time, the social stress began to seep into her schoolwork.

Unless it was sports day, of course. Vicky had natural talent. She didn't mind that the whole school was out on the field with plenty of parents watching.

Her first sports day didn't really go to plan. She was expected to win the running races because they had been practising all through the summer term.

She lined up at the starting line, excited and ready. The air horn went off, and she began to run.

She was in first position all the way until she spotted her mum in the front row, sitting next to Nina's mum. Vicky stopped and waved.

Everybody ran past poor Vicky. Ann shouted, "Run! Run!" Nina's mum was laughing so much. Vicky just stared, wondering what was so funny. She ended up last, but at least she finished her run.

Seven: Christmas

It was Christmas Eve. Vicky landed herself in trouble yet again. She buzzed with excitement. She loved Santa with her whole heart.

In her eyes, he was a big, chubby man who cared about her and wanted to bring her exciting presents.

Nobody ever gave her anything, so if Santa did, she must be loved. It made Vicky feel so special.

Each year, she always promised herself she would be extra good. She didn't want Santa to be disappointed.

She wanted her dad to wake up happy and enjoy the day. She wanted him to smile at her presents and maybe play with her. She prayed hard that night.

"Dear God, please make Dad wake up in a good mood. I would like a really big hug and want him to enjoy opening my presents with me. I hope I also get some. I have been extra good, so please make him play with me and enjoy the toys. Amen. Oh, and thank you for everything, including my dinner. Amen."

Presents were precious to Vicky because they could be taken away at any moment if John wasn't happy.

He looked for any excuse, being too loud, making a mess, or whatever he decided, just so he could confiscate them.

She knew her dad would come in to check they were asleep before Santa's visit. If John found anyone awake, it was Vicky who got punished, even if she wasn't the only one.

She learned to squeeze her eyes shut, face the other way, and not move for as long as possible.

That was the year she saw and heard her dad come in with the presents. She partly opened her eyes as bags rustled and footsteps came closer.

It confused her. She always thought Santa brought them to the bedroom. Why was her dad doing it, not Santa?

Vicky slept in the top bunk bed. Her father took away the large step ladders so she couldn't get out of bed and disturb them first thing in the morning. It meant she had to hold her wee all night too.

On Christmas morning she woke up bursting, staring down at the presents but unable to reach them.

Agnes woke up and went to the bathroom. When she came back, she started to feel all the presents, squeezing them and guessing what she might have.

Vicky's eyes filled with tears. She needed the toilet badly, but she also wanted to touch her own presents before they were taken into her parents' room.

Agnes wanted Vicky to join her, probably to compare sizes, making sure hers were better.

She also knew Vicky was brave enough to open one present, then hide it right at the back of her cupboard in case the rest of her toys were taken away.

At least she would have one to play with.

So, Agnes began piling her pillows and blankets on the floor. Vicky threw hers down too, including Ted, to make the pile higher. "Jump, Vicky, jump!" urged Agnes.

Within seconds, Vicky was on the floor. The pile of blankets toppled, and Vicky landed with a splat on the hard floor. Too busy to feel pain, she ran to the toilet, letting out a big sigh of relief.

When she came out, her dad was waiting. He pushed Vicky back inside and smacked her.

"I told you not to get out! You woke everybody up with your commotion," he said quietly, but angrily.

He walked her back to the bedroom, saw the mess on the floor, and gave her a second slap. He then picked her up and threw her onto the top bunk. "Stay there until I get you."

Vicky knew better than to say it was Agnes' idea. John turned to Agnes and said, in a gentler tone, "Come on then." He picked up her sack and off they went to her parents' room.

Through the walls, Vicky could hear the rustling of paper, followed by cries of "ahh, wow!" and lots of laughter.

All she could do was stare at her own presents from the height of her bunk, not knowing if her dad was coming back, or when.

Vicky's ankle was beginning to throb because of the jump she had just made.

She couldn't tell anyone. Her dad especially. He would just give it another twist to check she wasn't lying.

Her bum cheeks also hurt when she tried to sit, so the most comfortable way to lie was on her tummy, with her head in her pillow, while trying to drown out the noise coming from her parents' room.

Vicky had an idea to cheer herself up.

She was able to lift part of her mattress and could see her sister's bed below. Pretending it was raining, she started spitting on Agnes' pillow.

Tiny bits at first, then more. It made her feel like she had got one over on her sister.

At bedtime, Vicky found it hilarious when Agnes got into bed, complaining that her pillow was wet.

"Oh, just get in, don't be so silly, go to sleep. Christmas is over now. You can't stay up any longer!" said Ann quite tersely.

Vicky giggled, knowing her sister was lying in a puddle of spit.

Eventually, Vicky got to open her presents all by herself. Well, not exactly; Agnes kept a beady eye on her from the hall.

Christmas Day never felt as magical as she hoped. John started drinking as soon as he was dressed. "It's Christmas," was his excuse. Ann cooked all morning for lunch, then she started preparing a buffet shortly after.

Agnes played with Gwen, and when Vicky tried to join in, Agnes protested loudly. Vicky backed away quietly. She knew her dad would appear at any moment, so she left them to it.

That year, her presents were a game called "Striker" (a football game), a cowgirl dress-up outfit and a potato gun.

She had asked for the large doll that could stand up, walk, and talk. Her next-door neighbour had one for her birthday a month before.

She knew better than to expect the things she wanted.

Her dad would love the football game and maybe play with her at some point. As for the cowgirl suit, Vicky loved to play dress up, so anything was better than nothing.

Vicky was grateful.

They were presents, and to Vicky, presents meant someone cared. For now, that was enough.

Eight: Day Trips to Holidays

During the summer school breaks, Vicky didn't go away on proper holidays. Her parents took them out on day trips instead, normally on Saturdays. Sundays were kept for church.

Between the ages of five and seven, her parents always took the family to a nearby beach.

It was a paid picnic area covered with sand and grass, right next to the sea. To reach the beach, you had to climb over an extremely high sea wall.

The sea normally retreated for miles, but the tide could turn quickly. You had to keep an eye on it.

Streams would appear on the sand, growing wider and deeper until they could cut you off if you weren't paying attention.

Vicky's parents would sunbathe next to the car. Agnes had a sun lounger, and Vicky and Gwen had chairs.

Agnes stayed with her parents; she didn't like the sand in her toes. Gwen was too small to roam, and Vicky was happy to explore all day if she had the chance.

Vicky's parents would bring a packed lunch. When it came time to eat, calling Vicky off the beach was always a drama. John had to go looking and walk quite a distance to find her.

After lunch, the family would play on the beach. John brought kites, inflatable balls, a cricket bat, and a football.

If the kites came out, John helped to get all three into the air.

Vicky was good at it, so John attached a second string to hers so it could fly extra high.

Ann helped Gwen; she just liked to run on the beach with her kite trailing behind her, while Agnes wore a sour face because hers never stayed up very long.

John would hover around her, saying, "Pull harder! Let more out!" getting more frustrated with each word.

Vicky thought it was high enough; letting too much string out only meant she would have to wind it all back in.

"Oh, give me that a minute, let me show you," John would say, snatching the kite out of her hands quite roughly.

He'd play for what felt like hours. Vicky would ask for it back after a while. Her feet began to hurt from standing still, watching.

Eventually, she walked off to sit on the sea wall. But that wasn't good enough for John, apparently.

"Vicky is sulking, making a scene. She just can't share! Nobody's allowed to have a good time. She had to ruin a good day," he'd say.

She just wasn't that interested in watching her dad fly the kite and couldn't stand around.

If the inflatable balls came out and the wind picked up, they'd be blown into the sea or miles along the beach. Only Vicky was made to collect them; if she didn't, the next one came out of her pocket money.

Everyone enjoyed laughing at her as she ran after the ball. Bloody hell, those damn balls could fly.

If John decided on cricket or football, the balls were thrown gently for her siblings but full force at Vicky. They were often painful. John would laugh when he saw her upset.

He would pass it off as a normal throw. Vicky still remembers the pain from a sandy ball to the eye. It bruised for days and felt gritty for weeks.

During a cricket game, Vicky nearly broke one of her fingers when the ball made contact. Play stopped because her knuckle became swollen.

Once again, Vicky was blamed for ruining the game and was sent off to sit in a hot car while everyone else spent the afternoon on the beach.

There were other games John liked, such as throwing tennis balls at your ankles. If they hit you, you were out. It usually turned into how many balls could hit Vicky.

John told Vicky that she repeatedly ruined play at the beach and made her family miserable.

At night, she'd replay the day in her head, trying to figure out what she had done wrong and how she could do better next time.

How did that make sense? At school she was fast, sporty, and good at games. Nothing about her ruined anything.

Summer holidays had started as days out to the beach. Camping in the New Forest only came about when one of Ann's sisters invited her and another of her siblings to go camping with them.

It was the first holiday that involved more than just her parents and sisters. In fact, it was the first proper holiday ever.

We will call the sister who invited Ann, Yvette, and her husband, Conner. She was Vicky's favourite auntie.

They had three children, two boys and one girl who was the youngest. Let's call them Matthew, Alex, and Tia. Tia was a year younger than Agnes and the boys were a few years older than Agnes.

Ann's second sister was called, let's say, Anna, and her husband, Jack. She was the youngest of Ann's siblings.

They had two girls. One of the same age as Vicky, called Maisey, and a second was older than Gwen by a few years, called Layla. Three families with eight children, what could possibly go wrong?

As it was their first camping trip, Vicky's family had a small two-man tent. You could probably fit four adults in lying back-to-back.

The adults could just about stand up in the middle. John had borrowed it from his brother.

It had no windows and was totally dark inside unless you left the doors open. It was made of thick canvas and smelled musty.

Agnes and Gwen had camping beds, and Vicky was placed between them on the floor.

John and Ann went off each night to play cards in one of the other, larger tents.

They left the children alone, with no torches, listening to all sorts of noises coming from the bushes. They were petrified.

Camping in the forest as a grown-up, let alone as a child, with noises coming from the bushes, can scare just about anyone.

It's an experience to be tried if you have never done it. Forget camping in a field, it's not the same.

Conner had a trailer, and he would let all seven kids ride in the back while he drove over all the speed bumps on the campsite.

It was really good fun. The children would scream and sing as they went round.

John had seen the fun the kids were having, so he decided he could do one better.

He put Agnes, Vicky, and Gwen on top of the car on his roof rack and drove them around the same route. Luckily nobody fell.

All the other kids wanted a go too. Maisey and Layla's parents refused to let them do it. The same for Tia, but Matthew and Alex were allowed.

John refused and told them they were too heavy but got them to dangle off the back of the car as he drove around.

The seven kids, not counting Gwen, as she was about a year old, were allowed to go off in the woods and explore, as long as the boys looked after the girls, because they were the oldest.

They made rope swings and found a stream that was waist-deep in places that they jumped into. The girls were too scared to do it. Alex offered to hold Vicky's hand and became quite friendly.

When they all sat down, Alex said he wanted to show Vicky something. He took her to the other side of the bank and tried to kiss her.

Agnes was on her trail. She pushed Alex away, grabbed Vicky and said, "Stay away from him, he's horrible."

Vicky replied, "No, he's not!" She couldn't see the harm in Alex.

He had just been nice. Nobody was really nice to Vicky. She loved the attention.

That same holiday, the children met an ex-army man with his wife and son, who was just leaving his teenage years. The son loved showing them his army knife.

The boys told their parents. Their dad, with John as backup, confronted the couple about their son.

They were told he was mentally challenged, loved children, and was harmless. The men all had a beer and sat around chatting.

Later that day, the ex-army man built a death slide from a large fir tree.

These days this would not be allowed to happen.

You had to climb to the top of the tree, grab the rope, and hold. You glided to the bottom, where a springer spaniel jumped all over you.

Vicky hated that part, as she was scared of dogs. The men spread themselves out up the tree to help the women climb. Even Vicky's mum and Agnes had a go.

Next time they went camping, it was just Vicky's family, and it became a yearly thing, moving on from the day trips to the beach they'd had previously.

Nine: Locked in School

Vicky moved into her second year in school. Her new teacher was old and very strict; Vicky didn't like her very much.

She found herself daydreaming, drifting off to wonderful places, often getting the blackboard rubber thrown in her direction to bring her back to reality.

Vicky began to fall behind in her studies, and each day she slipped further until she no longer understood anything the teacher was saying.

She didn't know it then, but she might have been dyslexic. Nobody at school had picked it up. Her eyes could read the words, but her brain couldn't hold them in. She never would have believed she'd read a book, let alone write one.

She took each sentence carefully, repeating it until it truly made sense before she could move on to the next one. It was painstakingly slow.

Because everything took ten times longer to read and understand a simple sentence, Vicky became bored and she started to play up to keep herself amused.

Just before lunch, during story time, Vicky went to the toilet. She locked the cubicle and then climbed out from under the door.

The next girl who asked to go, came back jumping up and down, holding onto her privates saying, "Miss! Miss! The toilet doors are locked, and nobody is inside. I can't hold on any longer, I'm going to pee myself!" Everybody giggled and found it funny.

Vicky was sent off to get the caretaker; he needed to unlock the toilet doors. He offered Vicky sweets and told her stories on the slow walk back to the classroom.

The school caretaker was a gentle, friendly soul. Vicky wished he would just pick her up, give her a cuddle, and take her away from her life.

He reminded her of Santa, the image and fantasy she had made in her head. It must have been his belly.

Children normally start to walk home from school at about eight years old. Vicky had been playing on the street since she was about four.

By her second year in school, she was walking home by herself.

She was very streetwise when it came to traffic. It was about a fifteen-minute walk home for her little legs.

She needed to cross two small roads, with parked cars that blocked the view, and one major road that had a friendly lollipop man who had got to know the kids really well.

Vicky would often stop halfway home to stroke a husky. He was a big, fluffy white dog with a black tongue. The dog waited for the school kids to come out, just to lick anybody's hand clean.

One particular day, Vicky had been to the library with her class. A boy was sniggering about a book that had cavemen in it without a stitch of clothing on.

The boy got told off for being rude. Vicky became curious and decided she would look at it on her way out of school, just before she went home.

That way, no children or teachers could see what she was looking at. She couldn't believe the school had such a rude book, but curiosity got the better of her, and she just had to have a peek.

The problem was that the caretaker didn't see her squished in a corner, on top of a pile of cushions, reading quietly. School was over so he started to lock up.

Time passed, and Ann grew worried as Vicky was over an hour late. She ran to school to find her.

When she arrived, the school was locked. She hadn't spotted Vicky on the way either. Ann was now extremely worried, and panic took over.

The caretaker had heard her knocking and crying, so he came to see what the matter was. Between them, they searched the school, only to find Vicky on the floor with her head buried in a book.

Vicky was more worried about what her mum would think of her reading such a book, so she jumped up, threw the book behind her, and asked, "What are you doing here?"

Ann was so relieved to find Vicky. She hugged her and shouted at her, all at the same time.

Vicky was completely oblivious to what had just happened. The caretaker explained that school had finished over an hour ago.

I'm sure the caretaker found the book and replaced it back on the shelf. I wonder if he realised what Vicky had been looking at.

The school was putting on a Christmas show, *The Nutcracker, and* Vicky was a soldier.

Ann had the task of making all the soldiers' costumes. She was particularly good at it, and the school was very impressed.

Vicky did her part beautifully; except she ended up on the wrong side of the curtain at the closing scene.

Everybody was giggling, watching Vicky struggle to find her way through the curtain while a teacher whispered, "Vicky, this way."

She just loved to act.

That summer, John and Ann decided to try camping by themselves with just their children in tow.

The only thing Vicky could remember from this holiday was when she went for an ice cream.

Not far from the campsite was a plain, a flat piece of land in the forest; part of it was concreted over from World War II.

An ice cream man was always there throughout the summer. Vicky was lifted from the car and told not to run.

Vicky was wearing open-toe sandals, not really appropriate for the woods. Anyway, of course she ran to the ice cream van.

Horses always collected on this spot.

They were able to roam freely, whether because people fed them or because the tarmac was warm under their feet. So yes, there was lots of horse poo everywhere.

Vicky wasn't looking where she was going. She was concentrating on getting to the ice cream man as quickly as possible.

All of a sudden, she felt a warm squelch between her toes. She had stepped in horse manure, and because she had open-toe sandals, her foot sank right into the slop. Her foot was a mess.

I think you can guess how John handled that one. He was the one who had to clean it all up. He had to. There was no way Vicky was getting in the car like that.

Ten: Tied to a Chair

Vicky moved into her third year at school. Around this time, she started feeling sad. She didn't realise it was depression.

She spoke only when she had to and preferred to hide away in her room unless she was allowed outside.

She hated mealtimes. She couldn't cope with the small talk around the table, and when the conversation dried up, as it always did, everyone's eyes landed on her.

Agnes always started on her hair, then Ann joined in, and finally her father would throw in his two pence worth.

Vicky's hair was very blonde, curly, and frizzy. She barely noticed it until someone commented.

Ann cut it when she had the time, but from the few photos of Vicky, her hair stuck out in every direction, wild as Albert Einstein's.

Agnes always started with "Look at your hair, it makes you look like a…." (I can't use the word she actually said; it was one of those awful badges you got from Robinson's jam from the seventies, if anyone remembers. So, I'll say clown).

Then Ann would join in. "Oh, Vicky, it's a right old mess. We need to do something about that," she'd say slightly giggling. "People will laugh at you if you go out like that."

Finally, John added. "Jesus Christ, don't you have any pride? Do you want to live in the gutter? Do you even know what a brush is?"

Lunch then turned into a lecture about how she might as well be a street kid and go fend for herself.

"You don't deserve to have a place in the family," John would say. "We brought you up better than that!"

To be honest, Vicky didn't own a hairbrush, let alone know what to do with one. She had never been to a hairdresser; she only sat quietly watching while Agnes had a trim.

She wore Agnes's hand-me-downs. She didn't mind too much unless it was a dress. She hated dresses. They itched and made her feel uncomfortable. She couldn't be herself in them.

She hated most shoes since they were usually already worn by Agnes. Only plimsolls or deck shoes felt comfortable.

Agnes's school shoes always gave Vicky big blisters. Ann handed her plasters or popped them with a needle, saying, "I can't afford new ones. There is nothing wrong with those."

Vicky fidgeted and climbed everything. Her shoes were always scuffed at the toes. She was told off and made to polish them.

She got smacked a few times for coming home from school with them looking that way. She just couldn't help it.

On Sundays, Vicky went to church with Agnes, while Ann and John stayed home to make lunch. The vicar always asked where their parents were and told them to bring them next time.

They never went of course.

Both girls hated church.

At lunch, Vicky ate her roast dinner in silence. She hated it. She preferred it dry with no gravy. She liked to drown her plate in onion sauce just to hide the taste.

Her parents always gave her three fat Brussels sprouts. The bitter kind they had back then, or perhaps it was the way they were cooked. She was made to eat every single one.

She had a whole routine: cut each one into four pieces, fork it, hold your nose, drink at the ready, place it in, have a drink, mix together, and swallow.

Like most kids, she pushed food around her plate. Once, while doing this, she accidentally elbowed her sister. The table was high for her to sit at, which made her elbows stick up and out.

Agnes complained loudly, "Why are you eating like that? Move over!" and pushed Vicky onto the floor. John jumped up, picked Vicky up by her clothing, and sat her back at the table.

He then picked up the chair, with Vicky on it, and moved her to the very edge of the table, squeezing her legs together.

When she cried out, he reached down, grabbed one of Vicky's legs, and pulled it out roughly, placing it around the corner of the table leg.

John went off to the kitchen, grabbed two tea towels, and tied Vicky's elbows to the back of the chair with them.

It was so tight it pinched her skin, and the corner of the chair bars dug painfully into her arms.

Vicky felt humiliated. Both her sisters laughed while she sat there trying to finish her dinner. "Why is it always me?" Vicky thought to herself.

To be honest, it always was. Vicky never saw her sisters smacked or punished; she was the one who took the punishment.

It wasn't all bad. Vicky did have some good times, mainly what she made for herself. She normally found it with boys.

Stephen was her first boyfriend and Viraj her second.

Viraj was a sweet little Indian boy from her class. Vicky had been invited over to his house to play.

His mum looked like a princess; she wore such beautiful, bright clothes. Vicky was so impressed that she showed her wardrobe. She had never seen so many pretty things.

It turned out Viraj's dad was Vicky's nan's doctor. It's a small world.

That year, her aunt Yvette's husband, Conner ,died suddenly after being rushed into hospital with appendicitis.

Yvette left her three children with Ann while she went to the hospital. They didn't know their father had died.

While Vicky was playing with her cousins, Ann pulled her aside and said, "Conner has died. Don't you dare say a word to the others. When Yvette comes round, I need you to be brave and say nothing. Now go off and play."

Vicky walked back to her cousins with no time to think or process what she had just heard.

Minutes later, Tia said she couldn't wait to see her dad. She had a present for him.

Vicky felt like she had been hit by a truck. The air left her body.

She ran into the bathroom so she wouldn't burst into tears in front of them. She loved Conner so much. He was fun to be around. He couldn't be dead; he just couldn't.

Vicky wanted her mum to hold her while she cried, but she had to stay silent. It was breaking her.

Listening to Yvette telling her children was heartbreaking.

Vicky had to stand there emotionless. Watching them fall apart while she swallowed her own grief was one of the hardest moments of her childhood.

Eleven: Giving Up for Lent

Vicky was still in her third year of school. John was drinking heavily, and sometimes he even offered her a glass of cider.

It was Christmas when John poured a small glass of cider for Gwen, who was only two or three at the time.

Vicky complained because she liked the taste and wasn't allowed any. She had no idea it was wrong.

"You are an alcoholic," John said. "You are hooked on the stuff."

"I'm not," Vicky said quickly, and tried to prove it by not asking again.

She watched her little sister drink the cider until Gwen couldn't stand up and kept falling over. Ann and John laughed; they both found it very funny.

After the Christmas holidays, Vicky went back to school and started a project about Lent, the time when people give up something for a few weeks.

The teacher asked the class what they wanted to give up. "I am giving up cider," Vicky shouted proudly. "I don't like the way it makes me feel."

The teacher was horrified and called Vicky's parents into school. Vicky didn't know what was said in that meeting, but when her parents spoke to her afterwards, they seemed very calm.

They both told her to be careful what she said to people. Say the wrong thing and it could get you taken into care.

Ann said, "I was put into a children's home. It was horrible. Children were mean." She was trying to scare her. "They gang up on the new kids. You certainly don't want to be put in one."

Vicky was regretting what she had said now. "In future, don't tell anybody what goes on in our home. Okay, kid?"

Vicky nodded and was now careful about what she told others. John never offered his kids drinks again until they were adults.

At this age, Vicky shared a room with Agnes, then eventually swapped and shared with Gwen.

The room she shared with Agnes was very pink: the walls, curtains, and carpet. Vicky went to bed at about seven, and her sister Agnes was an hour later.

Both girls had bunk beds, but as Vicky got older, the bunks could be taken apart to become two single beds. They were moved and put on different sides of the room. Vicky liked this so much better.

At the foot of Vicky's bed was the window. At the foot of Agnes' bed was the door.

As the sun was setting, it would pour into Vicky's room, making it even more pink with a warm feel to it. She found she could truly relax for this one golden hour.

Vicky could hear children's voices while they played outside in the street. She listened intently, trying to work out who the voices belonged to. It helped her tune in to the birds.

Eventually, the children's voices would stop. The bird songs got louder, then eventually they stopped too.

Vicky knew it would be dark soon. Now all she could hear was the odd car and the television downstairs.

Eventually, Agnes would join her. Vicky pretended to be asleep, so she didn't get into any arguments.

Agnes preferred the dark and turned the light off before getting into bed. Vicky was scared of the dark, so when Agnes fell asleep, Vicky would turn the light back on.

Vicky's parents went to bed around ten. They would look in on Agnes and Vicky and turn the bedroom light off.

Once they had gone to bed, Vicky could hear their bed banging to a rhythm behind her head. She would turn the light back on until she fell asleep.

At night, Vicky felt more alone than ever. Everything she held in during the day came back even louder in the dark.

Her thoughts turned into demons hiding under the bed or in the wardrobe. Nothing stopped them, just like the real-life stuff during the day.

By morning, Vicky always woke up wondering what the day would bring.

Mornings were run like the military; everything had to be done quickly and exactly right.

And somewhere in between all that rushing, Ann would decide what chores were to be done and when, whether it was before school or at the weekend.

One job Vicky really hated was carpet cleaning day.

Vicky's mum didn't own a vacuum cleaner back then. It was a carpet sweeper, the kind you pushed across your floor.

Vicky's carpet was very flat, and bits of fluff would stick to it that a sweeper couldn't lift.

Ann would give Vicky the task of picking out the fluff. She wasn't allowed to pick up only what she saw; it had to be done military-style.

Vicky wasn't allowed out to play unless it was spotless. She was also tasked with removing her wall art made up of different shades, shapes, and sizes of bogies.

Each morning before school, Ann would bring up a mini electric heater so Vicky and Agnes could get dressed.

They didn't have central heating, and the mornings were chilly, cold enough to see her breath.

They had an open fire in the sitting room, but that was only lit in the afternoon.

Agnes and Vicky would sit shoulder to shoulder, kneeling with their bottoms resting on the backs of their legs. They fought over that damn heater.

The grill in the front was divided up into three sections; Vicky would make sure one-and-a-half grills exactly covered her legs. There was a bit of pushing and shoving because Agnes was trying to do the same.

It was so cold, Vicky didn't want to stand up and put her knickers on in case her place in front of the heater was stolen.

Agnes had to make the first move. She usually did, because Ann would shout up, making sure they were getting ready and weren't going to be late for school.

As soon as Agnes moved, Vicky sprawled until she was roasting ,and late, of course.

And then came wardrobe-sorting day, the one thing Vicky always dreaded.

Every year, Ann looked through each girl's wardrobe and swapped clothes around. Vicky hated it.

Vicky liked jeans, a T-shirt, and a jumper. Agnes preferred the odd dress or something Vicky wouldn't be seen dead in.

While Ann was busy with Agnes checking whether her clothes still fitted, Vicky was feeling pushed aside and became bored, so she picked up a metal coat hanger and started to play with it.

It was fun to bend the hanger into different shapes, but the hook itself was rigid and wouldn't bend no matter how hard Vicky tried.

So, Vicky had a bright idea and tried using her mouth. As she tried to bend it, it slipped, tore the back of her throat, and got wedged around her tonsils.

Vicky let out a fearful cry. Ann started to panic and rushed over to help her. Luckily, Ann was able to get it out. Vicky's throat was extremely sore.

Because of the fright it gave Ann, she grabbed Vicky by the shoulders and pushed her back and forth while screaming at her. Vicky was in complete shock and so was Ann.

Ann was a stay-at-home mum, though on the odd occasion she found work. The only job Vicky knew about was when Ann worked in a factory with her sister.

Ann did not stay there for long. But while Ann worked, Agnes and Vicky were picked up from school by John's parents.

They had a very large Ford Escort and later a Ford Granada. Both cars were bright blue and stood out from all the other cars.

Vicky liked being picked up from school because her grandparents were always right outside the front gate. It meant she did not have to walk anywhere.

The relationship with these grandparents was strained, but Vicky did not know that at the time.

The night before, John always told the girls what they could and could not say or do. Both girls did exactly what John told them.

John's parents leased a twelve-bedroom house. John and his brother had been born there. The people who stayed were permanent residents, ranging from young to incredibly old.

Vicky's grandparents made breakfast, lunch, and dinner for the residents and carried the trays over four floors to their rooms.

Agnes and Vicky were told to speak only when spoken to. They were also told to stay in the sitting room and not get in the way of their grandparents.

They could have the television on for an hour, then they were expected to do homework. Vicky did not get homework, so she used her felt-tip pens and colouring books.

The grandparents rarely came in, probably because they were preparing fourteen dinners, two of which were for themselves. Vicky and Agnes ate at home. It was the most boring place Vicky had ever known.

John's parents lived in the posh end of town. It kept them very busy.

Vicky and Agnes did a few things with their grandparents.

They took them strawberry picking more than once, although Vicky preferred to go with her other nan because she allowed her to eat more than they bought.

Sometimes, Vicky was allowed to deliver the dinner plates to the rooms with her nan. She was allowed to speak to some residents, others she had to hide from around the corner.

The stairs were very wide. The higher you went, the more the staircase wobbled. It was a very old, dirty house and smelled like a museum filled with stuffed animals.

Vicky's grandparents lived in the basement. It was cold and damp. When you visited, it made you feel like you needed to clean up as soon as you went home.

Vicky's grandad always had glassy eyes and carried a glass of whisky everywhere, saying "Yes, dear" to everything.

He owned a pellet rifle that leaned up against the wall in the kitchen. He used it to shoot pigeons.

Their back steps were covered in bird faeces, which made them dangerous to walk on. The smell there was atrocious.

Vicky was intrigued by the rifle and picked it up. She had never seen one before. John snatched it out of her hands and started shouting at his dad.

John turned to Vicky, shouting, "Why do you have to touch everything? Do you not know how dangerous that is, you silly little girl?"

John's dad said, "It's not loaded. She can have a look," and started to pass it to Vicky.

Vicky smiled and went to take it, but John smacked her around the head and said, "What did I just tell you?" John and his dad carried on arguing.

These were the grandparents who gave Vicky fifty pence every Sunday. Sunday afternoon or early evening was usually when they visited.

Vicky didn't get a chance to talk to them much. She was made to sit next to her nan on a sofa that had about a month's worth of food ingrained in it, while the adults talked.

Her nan loved to chat and spoke really posh. She would correct Vicky on the way she spoke, getting her to repeat words she had said wrong.

For instance, the word 'bowl.' Vicky would pronounce it bole (sounds like hole), and her nan would make sure Vicky exaggerated the letter w in bowl, so it sounded like bool.

She dyed her hair bright yellow. It was curly like Vicky's. She wore big glasses with bottle-top lenses and an old, worn-out pinafore dress covered in stains.

Twelve: Ballroom Dancing

Ann liked her children out from under her feet, so she sent them off to places like church. Over the years, Vicky went to things like Brownies, Guides, and ballroom dancing.

Vicky loved ballroom dancing. Agnes and their cousins were already taking lessons, so as soon as Vicky turned five, she joined them.

The lessons were in the town centre, and Agnes took her there by bus.

To begin with, Vicky had two left feet. Her dance partner was a boy called Kevin who liked to run away from her.

It made Vicky really cross, and she would chase after him for most of the lesson.

Agnes and Vicky had dance exams coming up. Ann asked Vicky to show her something she had learnt. Vicky was chuffed; her mum didn't usually take an interest.

Vicky did her routine and turned around to see Agnes and Ann rolling on the floor laughing. It upset Vicky a lot. She was only five and trying for her bronze award.

"Oh, Agnes, can you teach Vicky the basics of the foxtrot?" Ann said, half-jokingly, but disappointed. "I don't want people laughing at her."

Ann cut out some foot shapes, and Agnes taught Vicky the steps over and over again.

"I will get this and make my mum proud. I will," Vicky said to herself.

A few weeks later, Vicky took her first exam and was given Highly Commended top marks. Agnes received a Pass, two grades below, but she was doing her gold award.

Agnes was not very happy. She never wanted to help Vicky again. Over the next three years she completed silver, gold, and another award. Vicky was given Highly Commended for all of them.

Vicky was doing really well.

The teachers chose to partner with her, more than with the other kids, showing her how to improve her moves. Possibly because she showed talent and they wanted her to go far.

Quite often, she was offered a sweet for hard work. Something Agnes never got. Vicky was allowed to dip into a Quality Street tin, normally finding only toffees.

She didn't like toffee; it made her thirsty and her mouth dry.

There was a big, famous building where lots of concerts were held. A big ballroom competition was happening. Vicky was now six.

Vicky had been partnered with a boy called Dean, who was an incredibly good dancer. They were entered for the foxtrot.

Agnes hadn't entered anything. But there was a chance for a medal in some of the other events, so she also went along.

Vicky's cousins arrived with their parents, so Ann and John came and made a night of it.

It was time for the foxtrot,.Dean and Vicky got into position. They looked around and realised they were up against dancers of all ages.

Vicky thought she had no chance. John came to the dance floor, straightened Vicky up and said, "Don't let me down now, do you hear me!"

The music started and Dean took the lead. He was more experienced and helped Vicky keep time, even though he was the same age. When the music stopped, they went back to their parents.

Ann and John were too busy talking to Ann's sisters to notice her, so Vicky looked over to Dean and his parents. They were hugging him, and his family were all beaming from ear to ear.

Vicky smiled at Dean. His mum gave a wave and came over. She gave Vicky the biggest hug and asked her who her parents were.

Vicky pointed at her mum and dad, who had their backs turned, talking. Dean's mum gave John a poke and said, "Did you see what your daughter just did? She was amazing. Did you miss it?"

John turned abruptly and said, "Yes, she's incredibly good. She takes after her sister. She taught her everything she knows. She normally has two left feet."

Dean's mum's face changed. Oh no, Vicky thought... she knows now I'm not so good. Why did my dad say that? If we lose now, his mum will think it was me.

The smile disappeared from her face.

"Give credit where credit is due. She's done so well, you should be proud of her." Dean's mum said tersely, and walked off.

About an hour later, it was the judges' choice round. They were professional dancers from another country. Dean decided to enter again. His mum made him pull Vicky up. She knew they were too good to sit this one out.

Agnes also entered with her cousin. This time, John went up to Agnes, so Dean's mum came over to Vicky and Dean and said, "Good luck you two. Vicky, show your parents how it's done."

That is exactly what Vicky did. She came first in foxtrot and then first again in judges' choice.

John seemed chuffed once he saw Vicky's medals, which made Vicky smile. He even wanted to take to the floor with her. After their dance, he walked her around the room.

People stopped them to say how good Vicky looked and to tell her, "Well done!"

Vicky was a little embarrassed, but her father was in his element. That made Vicky really happy too. At last, she had done something right.

Vicky also went to Brownies, though not where the local children went. Ann didn't want her to mix with Tracy and Nina, so she found her another place to go.

Again, Vicky found herself walking there alone. On the way, there was one place she found really scary. A tunnel that went under the railway line at the train station. She hardly ever saw anybody there; it was dim and eerily quiet.

She would hold her breath and run as fast as her legs could carry her. It was even scarier coming home on a winter evening, when it was dark and badly lit.

Brownies for Vicky were just okay. She could take it or leave it. Most children already knew each other because they went to the same school, so Vicky felt a bit of an outsider. It was nothing new.

She made a couple of friends and eventually became a leader of a group. There isn't much more she remembers about it.

Thirteen: New Forest Holidays

The family were going on another camping trip to the New Forest.

It was the end of Vicky's third year of school. She had the odd day at the beach, but the forest holidays were the best.

She could take herself off for walks and be free from everybody.

Her imagination could go wild with tree folk, fairies, den-making, rope swings and paddling in streams.

Travelling from Vicky's home to the New Forest along the coast road took about four hours. The M20 and M3 were only partly built, so there were a lot of roadworks if you went that way.

The coastal road was better. There was plenty of scenery and wildlife to keep Vicky occupied.

The family would get up about two in the morning and stop at Brighton. It was halfway. They arrived around four for a coffee and a wee break.

John parked on the main road by the sea, in front of a few hotels that spread out along the coast.

It was deadly quiet at that time of day, but every year you could hear a vacuum cleaner in the distance. Vicky found it amazing that people at the hotel were up in the middle of the night cleaning.

John would go off for the first toilet break. He then waited by the heavily packed car while Ann took the children to the toilets.

The toilets were right on the seafront, a little walk away from where they had parked.

Just as Ann and the children left the toilets, two male figures started walking towards them. "Run! Don't stop until you get to the car!" Ann screamed, thinking they might cause trouble.

Vicky was extremely fast. She ran to warn her father about the two scary figures.

For once, Vicky got a pat on the back and was told to wait in the car while John went to find the others. Agnes could only waddle. She was slower and not very agile. Ann was weighed down carrying Gwen.

They all made it back to the car with the men still chasing. John puffed himself up, ready for a fight, but soon realised it was two police officers.

They had given chase because they thought Ann was up to no good. Once they realised children were involved and crying, they took John to the police car for questioning.

Vicky thought her dad had been arrested, but was relieved to see him get out again.

The police officers asked if everybody was okay and offered to escort them to the toilets if they still needed to go. They all had a bit of a giggle about the situation and then the police headed off.

In the car, Vicky was always given the uncomfortable seat in the middle, while her sisters got the window seats.

Vicky asked if she could have a window seat. She felt tired after all that running and wanted to lean against the car door so she could fall asleep.

Her father turned around and said, "Oh, I knew it, we praise you, but it never lasts long. Here you go again." He was already in a foul mood, tired and stressed from the police encounter.

"Why do you always have to moan? Next time we'll leave you behind. We can't go anywhere without you complaining. Gwen, give her the window seat."

He clouted Vicky around the head and said, "Get in."

Vicky wished she had never asked.

Her father chain-smoked the whole way to the Forest.

Not only did the smoke make it hard to breathe, but every time he flicked ash out of the window, it blew back in and burned Vicky on the face.

When they arrived, it was still dark. The children were told to wait in the car while John and Ann stretched their legs and looked around.

John parked the car facing into the woods with the headlights left on. The trees looked scary from the front window. It didn't help that the back and side windows were pitch black.

Vicky's mind ran wild, scaring her half to death. The bark on the tree trunks glistened, but the spaces between them stayed dark.

Vicky screamed. "Aaaah!"

She had watched too many *Doctor Who* episodes, the creepy ones that stay with you. Or maybe it was her recurring nightmare.

Her nightmares were always the same. Walking through dark woods, completely lost, trying to find a way out. The trees closed in and blocked her path. Her legs grew heavy and she couldn't run.

Vicky was half-asleep when she screamed. She probably woke the whole campsite and frightened Gwen, who was now crying.

Instead of comforting the children, John told Vicky off. This would give her father some ammunition to use against her later on in the holiday.

Before I go any further, I would like to explain something about Vicky's dreams. Numerous times, Vicky found herself in her parents' room, standing over her father's side of the bed.

She'd have that recurring dream and often sleepwalked to their bedroom. This startled John. To be honest, it would startle anyone.

"What the hell? Get back to bed. Now!" John would scream at her. Vicky was dazed.

Ann would jump out of bed and say, "She is dreaming, sleepwalking," and guide her back to bed. Vicky always fell back to sleep in seconds.

Vicky loved the forest, a world just for her. It was the one place where she could be alone in the woods, escape her family and enjoy the peace and quiet all on her own.

In Vicky's adult life, this place became particularly important to her. But while she was still a child, each time the holiday came to an end, Vicky would start bawling her eyes out, and something would die inside of her.

These holidays weren't free from torment. Vicky was still teased. She was such an easy target because she always gave them the reaction they were after.

As it grew dark, the family pretended to be zombies and chased Vicky. She would run into the woods because it scared her.

Vicky kept asking them to stop with a tearful, frightened tone, but they kept it up and repeated it year after year.

Everybody would be sitting outside the tent, looking up at the stars with hot chocolate, and every time Vicky came back, they chased her away.

It was not a game to Vicky; it had gone too far. The family found it funny and did this most nights. At least the woods became less scary now; it was her safe place.

Fourteen: A Pinky Promise

Along came Martin. It was Vicky's fourth year at school. She was around seven to eight years old now. They spent playtime together and sat next to each other in class if they had the chance.

For young children, they had an extraordinarily strong bond. In singing lessons, they were learning a song called "The Yellow Rose of Texas".

When the line "She's the sweetest little rosebud that Texas had ever known" came up, Martin would point at Vicky every single time.

It made her beam. Her first true love. That's what she thought anyway. Martin was the first person she ever started to open up to.

He felt really sorry for Vicky and promised that one day they would run away and get married. It was a pinky promise.

Vicky lived her whole life on the far end of the scales, the unloved end. She didn't know she was there. Why would she? It was the only place she had ever known.

So, when Martin was kind, when he showed her a bit of care, the scales didn't just tip, they slammed all the way to the other side. Right to the far end of the happy side.

Martin treated Vicky with such tenderness, something she wasn't used to. And when he talked about his parents with such love and warmth, she felt something wasn't quite right.

It felt like she was missing out. One thought came to mind: Do they even care?

One day, all this happiness got ripped away. Without warning, Martin changed schools, leaving Vicky behind, and it broke her heart.

She held onto the fact that he had promised to take her away and marry her.

Once she was old enough, he was going to find her and act on his promise. Pinky promises are never broken.

Martin stayed in Vicky's heart forever. She always wondered what happened to him.

Vicky came to realise she was finding her bits of happiness in boys. It wasn't long after Martin that she met Alex. Alex was the new boy at school.

The teacher had asked Vicky if she could help settle him in, and he was placed next to her at the table. She noticed he had beautiful blue, sparkly eyes that made him look so handsome.

Alex lived with his dad, older brother, and sister. No mum on the scene. He didn't live that far from Vicky, just a few back alleys away.

She would often meet up with him. Vicky's parents didn't know; they didn't really care.

Vicky was allowed to roam the streets until the streetlights came on. Alex liked to take her around the back of the church because he always wanted to kiss her.

His older brother was always telling him what he should be doing, and Vicky just didn't have a clue. They were only eight or nine years old.

Vicky loved to be away from the house. Nina and Tracy had moved on from her, especially while at school. They had made new friends now.

They still played on the streets with Vicky, but not as much as they once did. There was always some tension between them. So, if they could find someone else to play with, they would.

Vicky and Alex became boyfriend and girlfriend. It lasted most of that school year, until Alex wanted to look down Vicky's t-shirt — and the rest.

Vicky kept pushing him off and just wanted to go home, but she was in two minds. She didn't want to lose him as a friend. He was the only one she had.

She was hoping he would just stop if she told him off enough and kept saying no.

Alex started to get a bit forceful and said, "It's what boyfriends and girlfriends do, just let me."

Vicky started to feel a bit dirty and hated the feeling. She had to think fast. "Quick, the vicar is coming, run!"

Vicky ran all the way home and went up to her bedroom. Although nothing had happened, the whole experience put her off him. He was made of slugs and snails, and puppy dog tails.

The next day at school, Vicky told him she didn't want to be his girlfriend anymore. Alex found a new friend, so Vicky was back to being by herself again and started to regret her decision.

She started to miss his friendship. Vicky said to herself, "Which is better, being by myself or being friends with Alex? I may have to just put up with the way he acts sometimes."

She was only thinking of the good times.

They played games at playtime. They went looking for treasure in the alleyways and played on a pile of tyres at a garage.

She had so much fun. Vicky decided she wanted him back. Maybe he wouldn't do that sort of stuff again.

Alex knew all about the birds and bees. His brother had explained it all to him and even ribbed him for not doing the deed.

Vicky, on the other hand, knew nothing of the birds and the bees, so she didn't understand what he was trying to do.

After school, Vicky decided to walk around and call on Alex. He had the same idea, and they met somewhere in the middle.

He handed her a present wrapped with a bow. Nobody had done anything like that before. Vicky's eyes lit up.

"Open it then," Alex said eagerly. She unwrapped it to find a pair of second-hand earrings. Vicky was so happy.

She kissed him on the cheek and both their eyes lit up. He asked her to be his girlfriend, and Vicky eagerly accepted.

"Shall we go back to our special place?" he said. Vicky knew what he had in mind and told him, "I'm not allowed out for long, mum thinks I have gone to the shops, maybe after school tomorrow."

Alex was happy about that. He kissed her on the cheek and skipped off.

With her present in her hand, she ran off to tell her mum she had a boyfriend. She explained she had just bumped into him when he gave her the present.

Vicky thought it was about time her parents knew about Alex. She didn't want him just turning up on the doorstep, that would get her in trouble. Her parents hated school-friend visits.

"I think that present needs to go back, and tell him not to give you things again," Ann said tersely.

"What do you want a boyfriend for anyway? Only dirty girls have them at your age. You're not like that, are you?"

Vicky knew now exactly what her mum meant; was she a dirty girl? She wanted Alex as a friend but not the way he wanted it.

Alex didn't have a mother to guide him; he just had his older siblings. Vicky really wanted to ask her mum for advice but knew the only answer would be, dirty girl, get rid of him.

She played a lot with Alex at school, but after, she made excuses like she was grounded or had something else to do. It worked for a while until he turned up at the front door.

John answered. He went up to Vicky and through gritted teeth, he said, "Get rid of him. Do not encourage boys to come round ever again. What will the neighbours think?"

She tried to keep the conversation short, but he seemed to have his feet firmly fixed to the doorstep.

While Vicky was talking to Alex, she heard John say to Ann, "Get rid of that boy. She's turning into a right little slut."

She knew Alex had heard too, he had that look in his eye.

Ann arrived at the door and said, "Vicky is going to have her tea in a minute, she will see you at school." She then rudely shut the door.

Eventually, Alex got bored with Vicky because she was not going out to meet him. The relationship just fizzled out. In a way, she was glad. Alex could have got her into a whole heap of trouble.

Now, boys weren't always nice to Vicky, but that didn't affect her too much. She was playing French skipping with a few friends, when a boy named Taylor asked her if he could play.

She didn't like this boy. He hung around with a boy who always had snot coming out of his nose. Taylor was big and a bit rough too. You didn't want to get on the wrong side of him.

Vicky flatly refused, not allowing him to play, so he punched her straight in the eye. Now, she had a black eye to be proud of. It covered most of her face.

Fifteen: Itching Powder in School

In the summer term of Year Four, boys weren't on Vicky's radar anymore. Instead, she made friends with Dotty.

Both girls had been singled out to sit at a table and work by themselves on a different English comprehension workbook. They had both fallen behind, but it helped them become friends.

The girls were in a lesson learning how to sew with a needle and some wool. Vicky took her wool and tickled the neck of a boy who was sitting opposite her.

"Give me that, this is what you do," Dotty said. She took the wool and rubbed it hard down his neck; this gave him a type of rope burn.

The boy started to cry, and at lunchtime went home and told his mum. His mum rang the school to complain. Both girls got in trouble and were sent to Miss Loopy.

Vicky tried to explain she had only tickled him with it, but it got her into even more trouble for talking out of turn. She wasn't believed.

Vicky was having a really hard time at home. It was getting worse as she got older. To be honest, she hated school just as much, especially when it came to playtimes, trying to mix with friends.

Teachers could be stern just like at home, but there were a few people who showed Vicky kindness. The caretaker, for one, and a lovely dinner lady.

She had hair just like Vicky, blonde, curly, and shaggy. She was old and weathered-looking. She seemed to know Vicky, though Vicky didn't know her.

Vicky liked the kindness she showed and how she often singled her out. Maybe she was a distant family friend. Vicky never got to find out.

It was around her fourth year that Vicky started to stay for school meals. Dotty stayed, and Vicky felt like she was missing precious time with her only friend by going home for lunch.

When she returned, the bell often rang almost straight away, leaving little chance to play or properly join in.

This added to her already strained friendships. Staying for school dinners gave her more time in the playground, and the chance to bond.

Ann was happy for her to go because, up to this point, she hadn't really shown any interest in staying.

For school dinners, you lined up outside the canteen. When the doors opened, you lined up again in an orderly fashion to get your school food.

It was a main meal with pudding. Most of the time, Vicky liked them unless it was lumpy custard or semolina with a dollop of strong marmalade on top.

The canteen lady always gave Vicky the biggest piece of cake or extra, if nobody was looking.

The children sat at large hexagonal tables. There were about eight children to a table. Each one had salt and pepper that leaked everywhere, and a tin jug filled with water that was full of dents.

The teachers came over and filled your plastic cups a quarter full. It was never enough for Vicky. She was always extremely thirsty.

The school water fountains either trickled or had a slimy piece of gob on them, not very nice.

If you put your hand up for more water, the teacher would come over and refill it again, only a quarter full.

Vicky felt like that little boy from Oliver Twist, the looks he got were being given to anyone who wanted more water.

Vicky would normally put her hand up a third time, just as the jug was nearly empty. She needed that last bit. Sometimes it was only a dribble.

Drink bottles weren't allowed in schools back then. You just went thirsty.

The school food was really nice. Vicky only had very small portions at home. She was often told off by her dad for being a pig if she asked for more or anything else.

John was the only one who had seconds.

At school, Vicky always collected seconds. If food was left over, the children who wanted it could raise their hands. Vicky always did.

Vicky only stayed for school dinners because Dotty did. It meant they had more time together.

Dotty was raised by her dad. Her mum wasn't around, similar to Alex's home life, although she came from a very rich family.

She had a house five times as big as Vicky's, with a swimming pool and a sauna.

Dotty was troubled. She got into a lot of mischief with Vicky.

Once, while they were waiting in the canteen queue line, Vicky started to talk about itching powder and the joke shop. Vicky gave Dotty the idea, and she brought some into school.

Dotty could now put the plan into action. The two girls went into the toilets outside the canteen and put itching powder around the rim of the toilet seats.

After lunch, lots of children started to scratch their bums. At first, Dotty and Vicky thought it was funny, until one by one they were being sent to the medical bay.

Dotty and Vicky had to own up now. The teachers had asked everybody if they knew what it was, and to come forward because children were going to be sent to the hospital.

They were told they wouldn't be in trouble; they just needed to know what was causing it.

Vicky was worried and spoke to Dotty. "Why don't we say we heard from a group of boys saying it was itching powder, and we don't blame anybody?" Dotty agreed.

The teachers were grateful for the information, although they did ask which boys had said it.

In the afternoon, there was a boys-only assembly. I think we all know what that was about.

Dotty had an older brother and sister with about an eight-year age gap. There was an alleyway next to the primary school field that ran from the secondary school up to the pottery room.

In the lunch break, when they were on the field, Dotty would wait for her siblings. They were always smoking, and Dotty would ask for a puff too.

Vicky said, "I smoke too. When I went camping, my dad taught me how to do it." Which he did.

Vicky hated it because it made her feel ill. She hated the smoke smell because of the long car journeys where she was made to suffer it.

But of course, she wanted to show off in front of her mate. Her brother said, "Here then, take the packet, it has one left, and don't get caught."

There was part of the field you were not allowed to go on. It was an area teachers couldn't see. It had a gate at the bottom for letting vehicles in.

Vicky and Dotty went down there and lit up. Vicky had one puff and turned green; Dotty finished the rest. Luckily, Vicky carried sweets. They stuck an aniseed twist in their mouths and sneaked back onto the field.

The end of the school year meant another holiday, another camping trip.

While camping, the family went to Winchester for a day out. Vicky took her purse with her, hoping to spend the money her nan gave her for the holidays.

She liked to buy pen knives to engrave trees or make bows and arrows with, colouring books, sweets or ice cream — anything she was allowed to buy.

On this particular day, Vicky needed the toilet. John found a bench and sat with Agnes and Gwen while Vicky and her mum went off to the toilets.

Vicky finished first. She put her purse on the sink while she washed and dried her hands. When Ann came out, they went back to John quickly. He would definitely be moaning by now.

John had bought himself a coffee and one for Ann, and the girls were eating ice cream. Vicky asked if she could buy one. John said, "Give me your purse then, I will go get it."

Vicky reached in her back pocket, then tried the other one. It wasn't there. "Mum, Mum! I left my purse on the sink, quick, can we go back to the toilets."

John was really cross, telling Vicky how stupid she was. Ann grabbed Vicky's hand, and they ran off to the toilets together.

The purse was gone. Vicky was so upset. She had a lot of money in it. It was the start of her holiday, and she hadn't spent anything.

When they got back to John, Vicky was sobbing. John just laid into her, telling her how irresponsible she was.

For the rest of the holiday, she had to sit back and watch her sisters spend money on things, choose ice cream, and eat it in front of her.

Vicky had to go without. John said it was a lesson to her, not to lose her purse.

Sixteen: Reading a Room

Home life was still very hard. I just haven't talked about it much lately. I've mostly told you about Vicky's school world.

I need to go back now and explain some things that were happening at home around this time.

It isn't easy to put it all into a neat timeline. Those memories became jumbled.

Vicky was fighting her way through school at the same time, and everything blurred together, so some things aren't as clear as others.

But if we go back to the time Alex showed up on Vicky's doorstep, you'll see that she wasn't allowed out for quite a while after what happened with the boy.

She felt like she'd been sent to jail. It was torture. All the time she was at home, she had no peace. She was prodded and poked, bossed around, and made fun of by the whole family.

Her emotions were played with, and John loved to get a reaction.

She just had nowhere to escape. Her father took advantage of her emotionally without a hint of shame. The tasks he forced on her were over the top.

Making tea and coffee should have been one of the simpler ones, but the way he went about it was cruel.

He treated her as if that was all she was there for, to be bossed around, just like he did with Ann in the earlier years.

"Vicky, go make tea and a coffee for me. I don't want that gnat's pee you always make," John shouted.

"Why me? Can't Agnes make it? I always do it," Vicky replied.

John towered over Vicky, trying to intimidate her, baring his bottom teeth like he always did when he wanted to scare her. He snapped, "Now!"

When John spoke, you could barely see his teeth; they were small and crooked. Anytime he was mad, he bared his teeth like an angry dog.

Vicky was always on the lookout for them because it showed her he meant business.

Vicky had no choice, so she went off to make drinks for the whole family. It was extremely painful for her to make drinks for people she didn't like.

Agnes would come into the kitchen to wind Vicky up. Her favourite one was to dig her in the ribs so coffee and sugar would go all over the floor.

A lot of the time, her father would find some excuse, saying it was bad, and then just chuck it down the sink.

"That's disgusting. Your pocket money can pay for that wastage." This behaviour carried on until Vicky left home.

Vicky learnt to be hyper-vigilant. She could walk into a room and read it quickly. She knew exactly what mood everybody was in before talking to anybody.

And it stayed with her. As she grew, it sharpened.

She could sense people's moods, pick up on tension, and even feel when something wasn't said. She didn't always get it right, but most of the time her instincts were spot on.

On the streets she was constantly looking out for danger, and at home too. Now it was happening at school. Her parents had already changed the pathways in her brain.

At school, Vicky always scanned the classroom. It was her superpower. She needed to know what sort of mood everybody was in.

The thing was, she didn't even realise she was doing it, assessing for danger. It was her way of keeping herself safe.

As the years went on, Vicky had trouble falling asleep, and now it was getting worse. Every night, her thoughts circled.

She'd lie awake thinking, *Did I say something wrong? Did I do something wrong?*

She replayed the day in her head every single night, looking for answers. But an answer never came. It was just another pathway her parents had carved. Vicky had become an over-thinker.

When she played games, especially with her parents, she always lost. If she won by accident, she would smile and laugh and just be happy.

Normally, it was Ann who would say, "Now, I have told you over and over again to stop smiling at other people's failures. That's selfish, so take that smirk off your face."

She smiled because Agnes had such a sour face.

On the other hand, if she showed she was upset about losing, John would step in and say, "You need to learn how to lose, you can't win every time," giving her the look that meant, *don't you dare answer back.*

"You're such a sore loser. Go to your bedroom. It still has to be about you, doesn't it?"

Vicky just couldn't get her emotions right.

Seventeen: Jumping Off Garage Roofs

Vicky played in the streets every chance she got. It was a place where she could be in control.

No adults around to tell her what to do. No annoying sister making her feel worthless and stupid. The streets were a wonderland, one big place to explore.

She loved to ride her bike, play in the park, and go over to a pond to pond-dip.

She climbed walls so she could watch trains go past and jumped off garage roofs.

Her favourite thing to do was go on her skateboard, riding it down a slope into a car park. It's a wonder nothing terrible happened. She just didn't see the danger.

Vicky lived in a terraced house, which had a very small garden backing onto an alleyway. She used these alleyways all the time. It was her way of getting around.

Row after row, street by street, they all had alleyways. They were her secret tunnels, places to hide, to spy, to disappear in if another gang came charging down the street.

She was now about nine, moving into her fifth year of school. One afternoon, she found trouble, or trouble found her.

She was with her two friends, Nina and Tracy, when they came across another gang of kids.

These kids were climbing a garage roof and jumping off. They dared Vicky and her friends to do the same.

At first, Vicky and her friends didn't have the courage. It was quite hard to climb. The roof was flat and seemed extremely high.

The other kids started calling them names. Vicky ran at the wall and made it up to the second ledge, higher than the others had jumped from. "Do it! Do it! Do it!" shouted the other kids. She looked down.

"It's not that high," she said to herself, and jumped. She wasn't scared of heights, not one bit. It was the older kids who worried her. She needed to show she was just as tough as they were.

Pain immediately shot through her thin shins to her bony ankles, but she smiled through it. "Beat that!" she said, trying not to show the pain. She had learnt to hold pain in, and that now came naturally to her.

"Cowards!" she shouted. "Our gang is better than yours!" She beamed with pride.

Tracy and Nina wanted to leave, but Vicky had to prove herself. Her father was constantly telling her she was no good and loved to poke fun at her every moment he had.

She needed to prove herself to these bullies, to show she was actually good at something, even if it was jumping off garage roofs.

She turned to Tracy, the weaker of the two, and said, "Your turn, go on. I did it. You can't play with us again if you don't."

She was in pain with her ankles, so she didn't want to take the long ride home on her bike just yet.

It took Tracy a few attempts to get up on the roof, and she decided to jump from the lower ledge. That was fine by Vicky; she still wanted to be the best.

"Do it! Do it! Do it!" the kids chanted. Tracy jumped, landing on her feet with straight legs before collapsing in a heap, crying very loudly. Vicky felt guilty, knowing she had caused her pain.

"What's up?" Vicky asked, knowing full well. She could feel her own pain. "Grab my arm, and I will help you home," she said very sheepishly.

Tracy couldn't stand; the pain was too intense. Vicky knew she couldn't leave her and was feeling guilty.

She said, "Climb on my bike, I'll push you home. It's a long way, but I don't mind." Remember, they didn't carry mobile phones to call for help back then.

Tracy climbed on carefully. Nina had already taken off, probably when nobody was looking.

On the way home, Vicky tried to convince Tracy not to tell her mum. She started to imagine what her parents were going to say, especially if Tracy's parents came knocking.

In her mind, she was dead. Maybe she could run to her nanny Clara's house.

Vicky loved her nan, and she remembered her saying, "If your dad is mean to you again, come live with me." Maybe this was the time.

Vicky dropped Tracy at the gate and ran home as quickly as she could. She was relieved nobody turned up at her front door that evening. She went to bed early, wanting the day to be over.

The next morning was a school day. Agnes went with a friend. Vicky walked herself in. Yesterday's events felt behind her now. She felt relieved and skipped most of the way to school.

Soon after arriving, Vicky was called to the headmistress's office.

She beamed, thinking she must have done some decent work. *Mum and Dad are going to be really proud of me. Agnes is going to be so jealous, she chuckled.*

She jumped up quickly and ran to the office. Vicky knocked on the door excitedly, and stepped in. "Take that smile off your face. After your misconduct," Miss Loopy said sternly.

"Blah, blah, blah." Her words went over Vicky's head. *What have I done now?* Then she heard, "You must not dare people. If I told you to put your head in the oven, would you?"

Vicky tuned out again and started to imagine that phone call home.

Tracy's family must have said to Miss Loopy, "Tracy won't be in today. She was bullied into jumping off a garage roof. It's all Vicky's fault, blah, blah, blah."

"Crap! I'm in for it now," thought Vicky, worried she had brought trouble to her door.

The school phoned home, and Tracy's mum visited Ann. Luckily for Vicky, Ann was on her side.

She was mainly angry because the school got involved. She told them it happened out of school hours and had nothing to do with them.

When Tracy's mum went home, Vicky pleaded her case and told her mum that she hadn't made Tracy do it. It was the other kids.

This was her first lie. It made her feel awful.

Later that day, she was dragged to Tracy's house to apologise, which, of course, she did. The mothers began talking.

Ann started to get cross and raise her voice.

"Well, your daughter needs a backbone. Even if Vicky dared her, she needs to learn to say no. Weren't you ever dared to do something as a kid? Come on, Vicky, let's go. I think you should stay away from each other from now on."

Then Ann and Vicky stormed out.

It wasn't long before something else went wrong. Vicky was scrumping apples from a neighbour's tree. She didn't realise a boy in the garden was watching.

He was a little older than Vicky, a skinny, uncouth little boy. "I'm telling my mum you're stealing our apples!" he shouted.

"Come outside and say that," Vicky replied.

He opened his gate, walked right up to Vicky's, and repeated himself.

Vicky grabbed him by the hair and pushed him to the ground, right next to a nice little pile of dog poo.

Vicky said, "If you think for one minute of telling your parents, I'll shove this so far up your nose you'll be smelling shit for the rest of your life. Do you understand me?"

She was so scared of her parents finding out that she had to stop this boy in his tracks.

Over time, the other kids on the street saw Vicky as trouble and tried to stay away from her as much as possible.

She didn't have a clue why people didn't like her, or that her behaviour was unacceptable.

She had learnt to be aggressive with Agnes when she was mean, because it made her stop. Now Agnes was scared of Vicky.

Agnes still got her digs in when her parents were around because she had back-up.

Vicky was learning to use force to control or protect herself. She had no idea that what she was doing was wrong. It was normal to her.

She started to lose confidence.

Kids didn't want to be her friend at school. She began to believe her dad was right, that she was just a horrible person who deserved everything she got.

She became a loner, but she always had the boys. She continued to get up to all sorts of mischief and was constantly covered head to toe in bruises.

When she got older, she asked her mum why there weren't many photos of her as a child, even though there were plenty of her sisters.

Her mum said, "You were so accident-prone. Taking photos of you with bruises didn't look very nice."

Then she showed Vicky a few photographs she had of her, with massive bruises on her head, legs and arms.

They had happened at separate times and in various places.

Ann said, "You were always falling down the stairs, tripping over your dad's feet, falling off anything you sat on. You were so clumsy."

Vicky wasn't clumsy; she was particularly good at sports. Her dad, who played cricket at school, would always throw fast balls at her.

If Ann thought he was being a bit rough, he'd say, "She's normally so good. Have you seen her hit and catch a ball? She's also incredibly good at dodging. That's why I throw fast balls at her, just to make her better."

Vicky believed what John said.

It's what made her go back for more time and time again.

Did Ann believe it? Was it really just clumsiness?

Eighteen: Running Out of School

Back at school, Tracy, Vicky's archenemy and Dotty's old friend, could run fast. Vicky was always first in the summer sports day and had won a gold medal every year since her second year of school.

Tracy always came close but usually finished second or third.

Vicky was a bit scared of Tracy. She was bigger and could push her around.

As it got close to sports day in the fifth year, Tracy asked Vicky not to run so fast because she wanted to win the first-place medal.

Vicky agreed, because she was scared Tracy would beat her up. On the day, she ran her fastest time and, of course, she came first again.

Tracy was furious and told her she was going to get her older sister to sort her out.

Vicky stuck her tongue out and, at home time, ran as fast as she could in case Tracy's sister was waiting for her.

Tracy's older sister was in her final year of primary school. Vicky didn't mind the odd fight and could normally win, being a bit of a tomboy.

If she didn't, her dad would clout her for losing. Tracy's sister was big. And I mean big, tall, and wide.

Vicky always carried sweets and the money that her nan gave her. Tracy's older sister, Melanie, started making Vicky hand over her sweets. The odd one at first, then the whole bag.

After a while, she began asking for money instead. Then she wanted Vicky to bring in small toys she could hide in her pockets.

Eventually, Vicky plucked up the courage to tell her mum what had been happening.

She begged her mum not to tell her dad. He would say, "Just punch her, give her what for." Vicky couldn't because Melanie was so much bigger and stronger than her.

Ann told her not to worry. "If she does it again, just run home."

The next day, Melanie grabbed Vicky and shoved her up against the wall. "Where's my toy? And I want money. Give it to me now," she said. Vicky always tried to stand her ground but lost every time.

This time, she noticed that the teacher was up the other end of the playground with the boys playing football. She kicked Melanie in the shin and ran straight out the front gate until she was home.

Ann told Vicky she didn't need to go back and rang the school immediately. Vicky believed she was going to be in trouble again. Why hadn't she just given Melanie the things she asked for?

Vicky never saw Melanie after that, and the school never spoke to her about running out. It was sorted out that quickly.

A few weeks later, Ann told John what had happened. John started shouting at Vicky.

"Why can't you just do as I tell you? Smack her in the mouth. You're such a baby,.You're no kid of mine. I need to toughen you up."

Ann said, "Why can't you just leave her alone? She's been bullied at school, and she doesn't need it from you as well."

Vicky ran upstairs in tears. She could hear John and Ann arguing. She thought, "Why do I do it? Why do I make them row? Why can't they stop? Shut up! Shut up!"

She lay on her bed, holding Ted really hard. She put her pillow over her head, trying to drown out the noise. She was in for it later. Her dad would make sure she knew she was to blame.

A few days went by. Ann was catching the bus into town to buy Agnes new clothes.

Gwen wanted to go too. Vicky certainly didn't; she wasn't going to participate in giving Agnes compliments on everything she tried on.

Vicky only got hand-me-downs because John hated to waste money. Gwen got a mixture of hand-me-downs and new, probably because Vicky wore her clothes into the ground.

It was Saturday. John agreed that Vicky could stay at home. He was going to put some kitchen cupboards on a wall. "She can help me today," John said in such a cheery voice.

Vicky always wanted to impress her father, so she jumped at the opportunity to help him.

She had to hold the cupboards up while John screwed them to the wall. Vicky's arms were on fire, but if she complained or dropped them, her life wouldn't be worth living.

John was full of praise. It made Vicky want to do more. She felt really good that her dad was impressed.

John then asked her to help in the garden, pointing out that she was really strong. Vicky smiled willingly.

He had her doing all the heavy lifting until she was ready to drop. John noticed she was fading, so he sat down and asked her what had happened at school in a caring sort of way.

Vicky fell for it hook, line, and sinker. She let her guard down. She poured her heart out to him and then started to cry.

John's face changed ever so slightly. Vicky noticed this meant his mood had changed too.

He said, "I don't like weak little girls. Look at what you have done today, so why were you acting weak? I brought you up better than that. You need to toughen up."

John stood up and started to throw the odd punch at her in a fun, gentle way at first. Vicky stood up and punched back. She knew her dad was 'teaching' her how to fight and take it.

He wasn't teaching her anything. He just loved to knock her around. If she came at him with a punch or kick, he would say, "Harder, harder." As she increased the intensity, it made her wince.

John would smile and snigger. He didn't use an open hand to catch her strikes; he made a fist instead, meeting her blows head-on, which made her cry in pain.

Eventually, her dad would realise she had had enough. He would give her a tap on the shoulder, saying she had done well, then go on to say she still needed more teaching.

The next morning, Vicky's arms and knuckles were covered in bruises. Her arms felt limp, and she could hardly move them.

At breakfast, she told her mum, in front of her sisters, that her arms hurt from all her father's punching.

Ann looked at him crossly. John laughed, grabbed Vicky's arm, and gave it an almighty squeeze that sent pain shooting through her body. He said, "Let me see that. Oh yes, you have a few there."

"We were fighting," he said.

"I was showing Vicky how to defend herself. We had such a good time yesterday. She was so strong holding the shelves up. I was well impressed. Her left punch is getting better. She will soon have those bullies put in their place."

Vicky smiled from ear to ear and forgot about the pain. He praised her in front of her siblings. She was happy. Case closed.

Now, Vicky daydreamed a lot. She wanted to escape the world she was in. She loved looking out of the window onto the school field. She loved sports and was really good at them.

She especially loved the one hundred metres. She always came first at school.

Eventually, she ran against other schools. She was given a high ranking and went on to run for the Shepway district.

Mr Clarkson, a teacher in her final year, took her, as her parents couldn't make it, and she came fourth. She was quite disappointed with herself.

The school field was her favourite place. In the summer, towards the end of her fifth year, the children were allowed to play on the field at playtime.

She loved lying on it, feeling the sun on her face, birds tweeting, and the odd car racing by. The children's voices seemed quieter, or at least didn't bother her as much, when she was on the field.

Because Vicky could daydream like there was no tomorrow, she started not to pay attention in class. She often got the blackboard rubber thrown in her direction to bring her back to reality.

She began to fall behind in her studies until she just didn't understand anything the teacher was saying.

She became bored because she didn't understand the work. She started to play up to keep herself amused.

She was probably dyslexic. It had never been picked up in school or proved. She could read some words if she really tried but had trouble comprehending a sentence.

She couldn't take in the words she was reading. It took her ten times longer to read and understand a simple sentence.

Later in life, when she was studying for the exam that stood between her and the job she desperately wanted, she finally learned to slow down her reading.

She took each sentence carefully, repeating it until it truly made sense before she could move on to the next one.

It was painstakingly slow, but as the years went on it got better. Basically, Vicky taught herself to read in her twenties.

Recorder practice and choir were after school, and she went to both. She had problems reading sheet music, probably because of her dyslexia.

As soon as she learned one note and then they moved on to another, she forgot both.

Miss Loopy, the headmistress, taught both lessons, often singling out Vicky for being one step behind everyone else.

Normally, in recorder lessons, she would copy the person's hands next to her. She wanted to get better, so she practised over and over again.

John often got mad at Vicky. One day, he just snatched the recorder and threw it in the dustbin.

She went to practise and said she had lost her recorder. Miss Loopy gave her a spare to practice on in lessons.

Eventually, a letter was sent home saying they were moving on to tenor recorders. By then, Vicky had been borrowing one for months.

John bought her one, apparently not realising she'd been taking lessons at all.

Vicky basically taught herself the same way she did with reading. Eventually, she became really good at it. She can still play and remembers the tunes she learned off by heart.

The choir was something she also loved. She would sing to anybody who would listen. Agnes liked to hear her sing, often giving her songs to sing at night or in the car.

Again, she had a natural talent. Christmas was soon approaching. Vicky was hoping for the main part in her Christmas play, just like most kids. She was horrified to find out she was only in the choir.

She went home really sad and told her mum. Ann said, "Well, if you're not acting, I'm not coming to watch." This just added to her pain.

It all worked out in the end, as Vicky had a solo to sing from *Oliver Twist.* She became the talk of all the mums and children and won an award. It was a shame that her mum didn't get to watch it.

Nineteen: Dotty

Dotty was a latchkey kid too, just like Vicky. Dotty had asked Vicky to go round to her house after school.

They could go in the swimming pool. Vicky had just received her 10-metre badge, as her mum had left it quite late to teach her to swim.

That day at school, they had been given a form for a sponsored walk to help the elderly.

They were told to get as many sponsors as possible. People could sponsor them per mile. It was going to be a ten-mile walk.

Dotty told Vicky to get two forms, so she did. Dotty's house was about a 45-minute walk to the posh end of town.

On the way, Dotty was knocking on lots of strangers' doors, asking them to sponsor them because they didn't have anybody else.

They both got about 50 sponsors each. She told Vicky to use the other form for her family. Vicky said, "The school is going to be so proud, we are going to make so much money!"

They arrived at Dotty's house and went out to the pool. It was an outdoor pool but was covered in a poly tunnel to keep it warm.

Vicky didn't realise the pool didn't have a shallow end. If she couldn't put her feet down, she wouldn't swim.

Dotty realised Vicky wasn't swimming. She said, "Let's get out and do something else." Vicky was happy because she didn't feel safe and wasn't going to let go of the side.

Dotty's family wasn't at home; anything could have happened. Dotty gave Vicky a tour of her house. She showed her the sauna, but they didn't use it.

They went up this wide, large staircase. Vicky couldn't believe how big the house was. She was lost already.

Dotty entered her sister's room and looked for a packet of cigarettes which she found and then said, "Let's go to the shops."

She told Vicky to wait outside the shop while she went in and got food for their tea.

It wasn't long before Dotty came outside. She had stuffed snacks under her jumper, it was full. "Run!" she said. Vicky had a feeling she had stolen them.

Dotty denied it and said, "Oh no, I know the owner," but she clearly didn't.

They walked to a park that had a fishing lake. Dotty seemed to know all the boys fishing there.

She gave one boy, whom they called Half Pint, a cigarette in exchange for a light. Once the cigarette was lit, she offered it to Vicky.

Vicky refused because she hated the smell and had choked when she had tried it before. They sat in the park eating crisps, sweets, cake, fizzy pop, and milkshake. They ate it all.

They headed back to Dotty's house. Her Dad was now home. He caught Dotty and Vicky as they entered and said, "I need you both to wash up and then meet me in the study to discuss your day."

Vicky thought he sounded really posh.

He was dressed in a black suit, carrying a black briefcase he hadn't had time to put down.

Dotty knocked on these large double doors then had to wait to enter. It was all so strange for Vicky. Dotty's dad shouted, "Enter!"

Between them, they struggled with the big, heavy doors. They stepped into his office. It smelt very much like a library, and Vicky went quiet.

"So, you're Dotty's friend who came round to play. Have you had some dinner?" Dotty spoke for Vicky. "Yes, Dad, I sorted it all out."

"Ok then, maybe it's time you were off. When are your parents coming for you?" Vicky said, "They're not, I'm old enough to walk back by myself. I don't live very far."

Vicky lied. This was her second lie. She didn't want Dotty's dad to know she lived quite far away.

"Ok, Dotty, why don't you walk Vicky halfway back, so she is not by herself?" Dotty nodded, and the girls both walked out.

Dotty left Vicky at the football ground. It was getting dark; Vicky had to run, as she had to be home before dark. She had been having such a good time, she'd forgotten to think about going home.

A couple of weeks later, after both girls completed a ten-mile walk with the school, they decided to go door-to-door to collect their winnings.

Most people paid up, some didn't, and some just didn't open the door. Vicky had made quite a bit for charity.

Dotty said, "No, just hand in your family one. Keep this money, nobody will know." Vicky looked stunned and shocked. She had no choice; she didn't want to get Dotty into trouble.

She had no other way to explain how she got the money, so she kept it. She put it in her money box, never to be seen again.

Dotty and Vicky made a new friend called Loren. Vicky thought she was a bit odd, but Dotty liked her, so she tolerated her.

Dotty teased Loren, and Vicky joined in. It was better to tease than be teased. So, to protect herself she went along with Dotty.

Dotty invited everybody to her house to go in the pool. Vicky was reluctant, but both girls promised to look after her because they knew she wasn't a very good swimmer and would teach her.

Loren was in the deepest end of the pool with Dotty while Vicky held on to the edge. Dotty decided it would be funny to take off Loren's bikini while she was swimming in the deep end.

They fought for a while, and then Dotty swam over to Vicky to show her she had Loren's bikini.

"Chuck it in the deep end," said Vicky. She wanted Loren to get it back, but Dotty dived down and planted it on the bottom of the pool.

Loren was now naked. She was crying because she couldn't reach her bikini and couldn't leave the pool.

Dotty found it very funny. Vicky told Dotty to stop and pick up the bikini at the bottom. Dotty liked Vicky and always did what she asked.

They got out of the pool and dried off. Loren complained she was cold. "I can heat my sauna," said Dotty, eager to show it off. It was Vicky's first time in the sauna; it was really hot.

Dotty kept turning up the temperature, trying to make it as hot as possible. Vicky left; she couldn't take the heat. Loren stayed, trying to show she could take the heat.

Dotty decided it was too hot and left too. Loren said, "Chickens, I can stay here forever." Dotty got a bit cross, grabbed a chair, put it across the door, and sat on it so Loren couldn't get out.

Vicky wasn't very happy. Loren was forced to stay there a long time until she cried. Eventually, Vicky grabbed Dotty off the chair, told her not to be mean, and said she was going home.

Vicky tried to walk back with Loren, but now Loren was scared of Vicky too and just ran off. Vicky took the slowest walk home ever.

She was thinking about how mean Dotty had become. One day she might do it to her too, so Vicky decided never to be friends with her again.

There were a couple of bad incidents that involved Dotty. The first one was in Drama lessons.

Everybody was running around learning not to bump into each other and to change direction when asked.

On this particular day, when the teacher said, "All change," Dotty changed direction only to crash head-on with a boy.

Then she started to have a seizure and went into spasms in front of the whole class.

It was terrifying. Vicky and the class watched on.

A second teacher came in, and the ambulance men arrived shortly after. It was the ambulance men who asked the children to leave.

The school never addressed what had happened with the children.

Vicky had nightmares and was scared to go near Dotty. She kept wondering what would have happened if she'd had a seizure while she was in the pool or they were alone together.

It scared her for a long time.

Another incident happened about a year later. Vicky was going for her 400-metre badge for backstroke. Dotty happened to be in the pool at the same time.

Vicky collided heads with Dotty, which caused her to panic, and she couldn't pull herself back up to carry on swimming.

In the meantime, Dotty had been knocked unconscious, and a lifeguard had jumped in and pulled her from the water.

Vicky was drowning, or it felt like it, because everybody was focused on Dotty.

She saw Dotty vomit lots. Somebody had taken her swim cap off and caught her sick. Dotty came around dazed, and they took her off to a room.

The lady who was monitoring Vicky for her badge saw her struggling. She shouted, "Swim, Vicky, swim! You are OK, just swim."

Vicky was a few yards from earning her badge, and the woman wanted her to achieve it.

By this time, she was exhausted, thinking she was going to drown. Out came a huge metal pole; Vicky grabbed it, and she was pulled out of the water.

Vicky had no one to talk to about these two accidents involving Dotty. Every time she shut her eyes, she saw the images of Dotty over and over again.

Now, if you were wondering where her mum was while she was doing her badge, she was at home.

Ann didn't drive. It was an hour's walk to the pool, or she could catch the bus. Vicky always walked to the sports centre by herself.

Vicky had learnt her parents were never interested in anything she had to say, so she learnt never to speak to them unless they spoke to her first.

Twenty: A Lost Child

Vicky went to a few after-school clubs. She stopped going to swimming lessons, not long after the accident with Dotty. It made her scared of the water.

She started Guides. She found that more interesting. For a while, she was with her sister, and they all went on a camping trip, with four guides to a tent.

Agnes was the leader of a tent.

Each morning, she would drag Vicky out of her tent, while still in her sleeping bag and tip her out onto the damp grass. Agnes got the other three girls to join in.

Vicky still had fun, and Agnes didn't really give her too much trouble. The following year, Agnes left.

At the end of year five, yes, you guessed it, there was another camping trip.

Vicky had learnt to climb trees, mainly by her dad forcing her up them. He wouldn't let her give up until she made it to the top, even if she was crying because of the heights.

Agnes was too girly, so John never tried with her. Trees helped Vicky escape her sister. Gwen was fun to be around most of the time, now she was about four, maybe five years old.

One day in the New Forest, it was really hot, and Vicky had a bad migraine.

She couldn't lie in the tent as it was like an oven, and John didn't like the children in the sleeping compartment during the day because he worried bugs might get in.

So, Vicky found a huge tree to climb. It had a lovely flat bit where you could lie back and dangle your legs between two large branches. Feeling unwell, she fell asleep in the tree.

The search party was out. The family had been looking for so long that John and Ann decided to let the campsite warden know a child was missing.

Gwen was with Agnes when they found Vicky up the tree. Gwen found the whole thing amusing.

Walking to the campsite office with her sisters, Vicky saw the warden on the phone with the police. "We have found her," he told them, and then hung up.

Vicky's mum and dad had gone ahead, so when they saw Vicky with her sisters, Ann gave her a hug and said, "We were so worried about you, my darling," covering her in kisses.

Vicky found all this very strange. She had only fallen asleep in a tree.

Next minute, she started to throw up. She really wasn't well. John thanked the warden, gave Vicky a piggyback, and everybody started to walk back to the tent.

After a few moments, John stopped and said, "Get down. What were you thinking?" Ann piped up and said, "How dare you embarrass us like that? Get moving," and gave her a shove.

She walked on, lowering her head that was now pounding, throwing up a few more times on the way. Behind her, she could hear John and Ann talking about her in a heated discussion.

On arriving back, they put a blanket down on the grass under a small tree near the tent.

John gave Vicky her cardigan and said, "Use that as a pillow. Go and lie over there." She was happy to be in the shade and fell asleep.

One day, Ann took Vicky on a walk on her own and asked her why she was always causing trouble. Vicky tried to talk to her mum about everything she was feeling.

She tried to explain how Agnes was mean and was always trying to set her up, to get her into trouble, and about the way her dad treated her.

She certainly didn't mean, think, or feel the way her dad was portraying her to everybody.

She just wanted a peaceful, relaxing time. She suggested, she could go and get some help somewhere, like counselling.

Ann listened intently. Vicky was finally letting everything out and cried. Somebody was actually listening.

But after she had cried it all out, Ann spoke. "Your dad and I think it's not good for you to live with us anymore. You are clearly unhappy."

She spoke softly, but there was a tone Vicky hadn't heard before. It really unsettled her.

"When we get home, we will find you foster parents. Then you don't have to put up with us anymore. You're clearly not wanting to be around us."

Vicky cried and talked fast all at the same time.

"No, no, no. I don't want to leave. I just want everybody to stop picking on me. Believe me when I say I have headaches. I want you to understand

I don't start the arguments. If people just left me alone, I would be really quiet, you wouldn't even notice I'm there. I don't need to go into foster care."

The words were falling out of her mouth. She was extremely upset.

Ann calmly said, "Well, we can't all go on like this anymore. You need to change. You have one more chance. Stop overreacting to what people say, just stay quiet and don't answer back. I need to see a change in you."

Vicky promised she would. She could do this; she had to change so she would not be taken away.

She thought, *"Why do I react when nobody else does? Why can't I be normal? What is it I'm doing that I get smacked for, that my sisters don't? I need to change. Fast!"*

Twenty-One: Denise, a True Friend

In primary school, there were two classes per year.

Vicky and Nina were in one, and Tracy was put in the other. You'll remember that both girls were Vicky's very first friends, and lived on the same street.

Although they played together outside, Vicky didn't really mix with Tracy at school.

During after-school activities, both classes mixed, and Vicky made a friend called Denise from Tracy's class.

Vicky was now in her sixth year of school, which would be year five today.

School years were numbered differently back then because there was no reception year; it was called year one.

Denise was really good for Vicky; she helped her to stay grounded. Denise's friends often let her down, so they needed each other.

Denise lived in the same group of houses, but several alleyways away. She was probably her furthest-away friend. Their friendship really blossomed after Denise's mum rang Ann.

Vicky's mum now had a landline. Denise's mum asked if Vicky could sleep over. It was Denise's birthday treat, and her two main friends had let her down.

Ann agreed and told Vicky to be back home by midday tomorrow. Both girls were excited.

Denise had a lovely black-and-white Border Collie that followed her everywhere and just wanted to be cuddled.

Vicky and Denise fancied a trip to the park. Her dog knew as soon as Denise put her shoes on. He wagged his tail and jumped up and down.

Vicky wasn't so keen when he was a bit boisterous, but Denise always sensed how she was feeling and corrected her dog straight away.

In this special park, which Vicky didn't visit very often, a small stream ran through it.

It had a wooden walkway beside it. The dog saw a baby pigeon struggling in the stream and jumped into the water after it.

Denise called her dog back and climbed into the stream to retrieve it. The bird looked sick, so Vicky took off her jumper and wrapped the baby pigeon up snugly inside it.

"It needs food," Denise said.

"I know," said Vicky. "I have an auntie not too far from here. We could take it to her, and she will know what to do."

Vicky's auntie was not too pleased with the scruffy, diseased little thing, as she called it. She told them to put it in the garage and said there were plenty of cardboard boxes they could use.

Vicky placed her jumper and the bird into a box, offered it some bread that her Auntie gave her, and left it in a corner to recover.

A few days later, Vicky's mum said, "Where's your jumper?" Vicky realised where she had left it.

"Oh, can I go to Auntie's house? I left my jumper there. I can go now and check on the bird and bring my jumper back. Do you have an old towel I could use?" She said excitedly.

Ann replied, "Your jumper must be ruined. What were you thinking, giving it to a smelly bird? Your uncle strangled its neck and killed it. He didn't want it in his garage."

Vicky ran off to her bedroom, really upset.

"That's another thing I have killed," she thought to herself. It reminded her of her cat. "I should have let Denise take it home, she would have cared for it properly. How will I tell Denise this sad news?"

It wasn't long after the pigeon died that Denise came calling. "Quick, get your shoes on and come to my house, I have something to show you." Vicky couldn't get out of her house quickly enough.

They ran to Denise's house. Vicky was holding the dog's lead, which helped pull her along the road. Denise took her straight out to her garden shed.

Vicky's face beamed. It was enormous; she had never seen a big bird up close. "Where did you get it?" She said, looking surprised.

Denise explained carefully, making sure she didn't forget anything, because she knew Vicky would ask a million questions otherwise.

"It's been in my garden for days. Its parents were nearby, but one day they just didn't come back. My mum told me to leave it alone to see if its parents would come back, but they didn't.

"It started to look very weak, so my dad made a box for it, and I have been feeding it every day. Do you want to have a go?"

Vicky was around at Denise's house every day until that little seagull grew up and flew off. Denise's parents fed Vicky every night too. She had never eaten so much food before.

Her parents just didn't feed her if she wasn't home at the right time.

Vicky was always late and being told off most nights, but she didn't care; she was going to help this bird, and nobody was going to stop her.

School life was better now she had found Denise; it was just a shame they were in different classes.

This year, on the camping trip, Vicky ended up in hospital. She loved to be barefoot. She hated the feel of shoes and preferred to wear none.

The campsite was in a woodland. There were twigs everywhere.

Vicky was walking barefoot to collect water. Somehow, a twig as thick as an adult's little finger went through the ball of her foot and got stuck.

John and Ann had to take her to the hospital, where it was removed, and Vicky had a tetanus injection.

The Drive home was always sad. Vicky would sing songs she learnt at primary school in the car if she was allowed. Her sisters loved to add different words to the song to put her off. An argument broke out, with Vicky's voice being the loudest.

John stopped the car, pulled Vicky out across and over Gwen, smacked her three times in front of her sisters, then put her back in the car and said, "I want silence for the rest of the way home."

She knew not to cry or react. It was the best way to get it over with.

Agnes gave her a dig in the ribs and pulled a face. She whispered, "How's your bum?" Vicky didn't react.

Car journeys normally caused Vicky a lot of problems.

She hated sitting so close to her sisters and the cigarette smoke always made her quite ill. If someone were to be sick in the car, it was normally Vicky.

Twenty-Two: John's World

Vicky didn't know much about John's life; everything she did know was what Ann told her.

John was brought up in a guest house and had a brother about four years younger than him.

They both went to a private school in their primary school years. John learnt to play cricket and later joined a team at secondary school.

He eventually moved to a public school because his parents couldn't afford the private fees any longer.

Because he spoke in a posh way, he was bullied, and later Ann's family laughed at him.

He once threw his brother into a bank of stinging nettles, simply because he didn't like him.

Vicky guessed his parents didn't have much time for him either. They must have been too busy with the guest house. During and after the war, they had soldiers staying in their rooms.

John's working life started in a small shop. That's where he met Ann.

Later, he got a job in a larger shop and worked his way up to become manager of an area that covered London and a lot of the southeast.

Vicky went to work with her dad a few times in the school holidays, especially when he went to London.

Ann would often make him take her. He was reluctant because he didn't know how his boss would react if he ever found out.

Vicky spent most of her day in the staff room. Her dad would buy a newspaper for himself and a magazine for Vicky. She always packed her colouring book too.

Sometimes, when she was really bored, she would go into the shop and ask for something to do.

She would unpack things and stack them onto the shelves, and sometimes the staff took Vicky up to the shops to buy a drink and biscuits for everybody.

One particular day, a regional manager with two other colleagues came to visit Vicky's dad while he was at one of the London shops. Vicky had gone to work with him that day.

John looked worried. He had about ten minutes to decide what to do with Vicky before they arrived.

Eventually, he saw a cupboard in the staff room. It was just big enough for Vicky to hide in.

He put her in there with all her books and said, "If they find you, I will lose my job. You stay there, you don't move, you don't make a sound. If you let me down, you get the biggest hiding, do you hear me?"

Vicky sat in that cupboard, knees to her chest for quite some time, scared she would be found.

She was in there long enough for her dad to have a meeting and show them around. They even made tea above Vicky's head.

When Gwen got a bit older, the whole family would go to London. John would go to work, and Ann, Agnes, Vicky, and Gwen would catch the tube and go around London for the entire day.

Although Vicky liked to see the sights, her legs hurt from all the walking. It also got extremely hot visiting museums. Being hot and having to carry your coat all day was not Vicky's type of fun.

By the end of the day, she was tired, thirsty, hungry, and in a grumpy mood. Ann would complain to John that Vicky had complained all day.

Vicky knew a few smacks were on the cards, but she just didn't care. She just wanted to go home to rest.

She had been up since 5am to get ready and be in London for 8am, had walked all day, and was back in the car about 6pm.

Ann loved London and liked to go up every chance she got. Gwen was in a pushchair, so it was easy for her.

The pushchair was loaded up. Agnes would help her push it, so anything Agnes carried went on the pushchair, but Vicky had to carry all her stuff, including her packed lunch.

Another time, Vicky went to London with her dad. A young man, who was a staff member, asked whether Vicky wanted to go back to his house for lunch.

He said his mum would feed her and she could play with the puppies. Vicky was excited, and her dad said she could go but must behave.

On arriving at this man's house, a large pit bull came pounding down the stairs straight for Vicky, jumping all over her. Vicky screamed and cried.

The guy took the dog upstairs and said to Vicky, "Come and see the puppies." Vicky bent down next to them, but again they started to jump and bite at her.

Vicky really didn't like it, so he took Vicky upstairs and gave her some beans on toast. When the man got back to work, he told John that she had screamed and cried at the puppies.

On the way home, Vicky's dad laid into her. She had embarrassed him, so he was mad. For the whole weekend, he had her working for him all day as punishment.

He told her she needed to toughen up, and was an embarrassment, and gave her the odd clout when he felt like it.

Another of John's work colleagues had a toy poodle that she brought to work. It sat in the shop window and brought the customers in. Its owner was an older lady who had just lost her husband.

The dog had never been left before; it was well behaved, so they allowed her to bring it to work. This lady told John the best thing you can do to stop your children from fearing dogs is to get one.

She was off to a wedding and was going to put her dog in kennels but was reluctant. If John wanted to look after her dog for the weekend he could, she said.

So one evening, without telling anyone, John turned up with a toy poodle, a real dog.

Vicky was excited but nervous and said the dog could sleep in her room. She liked her friend's dog, but it scared her if it jumped or mouthed at her.

This dog was small, really soppy and cute. It was so gentle, Vicky took to it straight away. She played with it all evening, and when it was time for bed she went up alone.

John said when they go to bed, he would put it in her room because he had to let it out last thing for a wee.

By ten o'clock, Agnes was asleep. John brought in the basket for the dog to sleep in and whispered to Vicky, "He's not to be played with."

Vicky rolled over, quite sleepy, and said, "Okay Daddy." The dog was placed in its bed, and John left and shut the door.

Vicky hated the dark, and now something was clawing at her bed. She was too scared to turn the light on, so instead she shouted out for her dad.

John came in very cross, and said, "Are you trying to wake the bloody neighbourhood? You've scared that poor dog!" It was hiding in a corner.

Before Vicky could explain, the dog was picked up and taken to John's room and placed on the dressing table in its box, where it slept all night.

When John reunited the dog with its owner, he told her the dog had kept him up all night long, but apart from that, everybody loved him.

The owner said the dog slept on her bed and hadn't thought to tell John. This was when he decided he wanted to get a dog.

The lady from the shop gave John the phone number of where she had got her dog from.

It was a place up in Scotland. The breeder had arranged for a lorry to meet John just outside the Port of Dover.

Vicky was allowed to go with him; he needed someone to hold on to the dog for the journey home. Vicky was still slightly scared of dogs, but the rest of the family were more scared.

The lorry driver had a long chat with John; Vicky was getting very impatient.

She could see the cardboard box but nothing else. The driver said she had travelled well and eventually passed the box down to Vicky.

Vicky held on tight. The box wasn't sealed, just flapped over, and this tiny bear-looking face popped out. It was so tiny. Vicky melted and didn't feel scared anymore.

As soon as John and Vicky returned to the car, John lifted the dog out, gave it the once-over and handed it to Vicky. Vicky couldn't have been happier; her heart was melting.

On returning home, Ann, Agnes and Gwen were all very scared of the dog. Ann was terrified of dogs and showed it by her reactions to her children. They therefore learnt dogs were something to fear.

Vicky, being a little braver, had to keep chasing after it to keep it away from everybody else when it got too silly.

Ann was really scared. She made Agnes and Gwen more nervous. John thought of Brandy as a name and it stuck, so Brandy slept in John's bedroom, in a box on top of a chest of drawers.

For the first few months, while Vicky was off school, she was in sole charge of looking after Brandy.

Twenty-Three: Brandy the Guard Dog

John and Ann gave Agnes her own room at the back of the house, and Gwen moved in with Vicky.

Vicky was much happier with this arrangement. She definitely didn't want the back room. It was very dark at night, and when you looked out the window, it faced the back alley.

Vicky had been moved into a back bedroom before because she'd had an ear infection and wasn't very well. Agnes was sleeping with Gwen in the other room.

One night, Agnes came sleepwalking into Vicky's room. She shook Vicky awake with her hands around her neck, mumbling that there was a fire and they had to get out.

Agnes was dreaming, and Vicky woke up to being strangled by her. Vicky was petrified and never slept properly again.

Every time Vicky got up to use the bathroom, after Agnes moved into the back bedroom, she could hear Agnes mumbling through the wall.

Vicky was scared and thought she was going to come after her again, so she locked the bathroom door and screamed for her parents.

Every time she did this, she woke the whole household up, and John would have to get up. He was always furious.

Vicky's room, which she shared with Gwen now, was also at the back, but it was set further back.

She had light coming in from her own kitchen and her neighbours' kitchen, which made it feel less frightening.

Now Gwen was going to bed at 7pm, Vicky at 8.30pm, and Agnes at 10pm. Vicky wasn't happy that Agnes was allowed to stay up and watch *The Professionals*, a cop series on the television.

Vicky had to go to bed as soon as *Coronation Street* finished.

That theme tune haunts Vicky to this day. She would try to stay up, saying she was listening to the theme tune. But John would spell out B E D while showing his teeth.

Vicky knew when she had pushed too far. Next would be a slap, so she slowly edged towards the door, staring at the television.

Gwen was always asleep when Vicky went to bed, and she wasn't mean like Agnes.

She was five years younger than Vicky. She might join Agnes, Ann, and John against Vicky, but she didn't know any different.

Brandy was allowed to sleep in Vicky's room. John said he couldn't cope with the dog staring at him all night. By now, Vicky wasn't scared of Brandy at all.

That first night, Vicky picked Brandy up onto her bed, and that's where she stayed until Vicky was old enough and left home.

Brandy liked to bury herself under the covers and then wriggle out and sleep on top of Vicky when she got too hot.

Vicky started to train Brandy. She taught her to sit, stay, beg, come, and heel.

John and Ann were quite impressed when they took her out. She was never put on a lead because she walked to heel and came when called.

Vicky loved to teach her dog lots of things. Brandy was quite clever. The family had all stopped being scared of dogs, except Agnes. Vicky planned to use this to her advantage.

She taught Brandy to bark and chase people on the word 'attack.' She got Gwen to help, by saying she was training her up to be a guard dog.

Gwen was starting to look up to Vicky and followed her everywhere.

The next time Agnes was mean, Vicky shouted "attack", and Brandy ran to Agnes, barking. Agnes was would scream and run off, with Brandy chasing after her.

John and Ann thought it was very funny, and so did Vicky. Brandy stole socks, too.

She loved to grab them when you tried to put your socks on in the morning. It was impossible to take them off her until she lost interest.

Ted the teddy bear had lost his appeal now; she had Brandy.

Brandy also became her bodyguard. She hated anyone touching Vicky. If John hit Vicky, Brandy was right there, in between, barking at John. She tried to nip him once or twice.

John was never mean to Brandy. He found her funny, and it distracted him from hitting Vicky. He'd just pick her up while she tried to nip him and move her to a different room.

When she nipped, it didn't hurt; she never bit hard.

Vicky's life had got slightly better. She had a friend in Gwen, who liked to go out and play with Vicky and her friends.

Vicky's friends had brothers and sisters, so there were more children she could hang around with.

One day, Vicky was on the streets playing chase. One of the small boys chased Gwen into the road; a car stopped very quickly.

An old man got out of his car, came over to Vicky and started telling her off. Probably because she was one of the oldest.

She tried to tell him it wasn't her who chased Gwen into the road, but he wasn't interested. The other kids started smiling and laughing, which made this poor man even madder.

Eventually, he drove off, and Vicky gave him the two-finger salute.

That evening, Gwen told everybody what happened at the dinner table because she found it all very funny.

John and Ann didn't. Ann pulled Vicky from the table and screamed at her, saying, "You could have killed her. I wish that car had hit you, you wouldn't be laughing now."

Vicky started to cry while trying to defend herself. Trying to say she wasn't the one who chased her. They just didn't care.

John saw that everything was getting out of control. The children were crying, Ann in a fit of rage, and Brandy barking as loud as she could.

John grabbed Vicky and dragged her up to her room. He took off his trouser belt and gave her one strike. Vicky screamed in pain, and John clamped his hand over her mouth.

"That's how my dad knocked me down a peg or two. If you don't start acting the way you should, this is what I will use in future. Do you hear me?" Vicky nodded, with tears running down her face.

John left Vicky's room and collected Brandy. He gave her to Vicky and said, "You can stay there until morning. I don't want to see that ugly little face of yours." Then he left.

Vicky was in complete shock, not sure what she had really done. She sat on her bed, then jumped up immediately. The pain from the belt whip was so intense that it shot through her whole body.

She lay down carefully. Brandy licked all her tears and bogies away. This was one of the worst beatings, pain-wise, Vicky ever had.

When Gwen came to bed, she brought a cake for Vicky. She had sneaked it from her plate and gave it to her with a big hug.

"I'm so sorry Vicky. That wasn't even your fault." Vicky smiled. "It's not your fault either. Can you sing to me so I can fall asleep?" And that's what Gwen did.

Gwen was still allowed to go out to play with Vicky. She learnt not to tell her parents anything about their day, and Vicky learnt to look after Gwen a little more carefully.

Sometimes Gwen and Vicky just went out to play together, with no other friends. Vicky preferred that.

Gwen was a bit like Vicky, she loved adventures, and Vicky was good at making them happen.

They took chalk out and made a treasure trail to follow, as well as hopscotch. They rode their bikes quite far and found unfamiliar places to explore.

They also decorated the shed and told Ann they were going to sleep out there as soon as it was dark. That night, both girls came running in saying they heard someone in the alleyway, which the shed backed onto. But hey, they still had fun setting it all up.

Gwen and Vicky bonded well, to the point they could even be left playing board games together, which they both loved.

Agnes was quite a serious type of girl and normally just hung around her mum. She was the golden child.

Vicky loved Gwen, but she also needed time to herself. She loved to swing. She had one in her garden and could go really high.

She sneaked out to the park every now and again when Gwen was busy and used the swings there, just to be by herself.

Vicky was doing better now at primary school. She had a couple of friends. Boys, well, she had given up on them, but they still asked her out, and she still attracted a lot of attention.

By her sixth year in primary school, age ten, reading was ramping up.

Everybody was asked to choose a book. When you finished reading it, you had to go to the teacher, who questioned you about it, and then you could exchange it.

Vicky kept her book for months. She could read words but couldn't understand what she had just read.

This teacher was extremely strict, and Vicky was too scared to tell her she couldn't read it, for fear of getting into trouble.

After a few months, this teacher left. She died from a brain tumour quite suddenly, and Vicky was disturbed by it.

She felt a bit guilty because her new teacher never wanted a rundown on the book she had just read, so she could simply exchange it now.

She was partly relieved that the other teacher had left, and that was what made her feel guilty.

In English lessons, she had to read over and over again until she understood the question. She was terribly slow and rarely finished her work.

She was told off a lot for chatting and not finishing her work. This wasn't the case; she just struggled to read.

Vicky liked maths, it was interesting to her, and of course, arts and crafts. She also loved PE. She was particularly good at that.

Twenty-Four: Horse Riding

School holidays had now arrived, and this year, Vicky packed a lot in.

First, she went camping with the Guides. This time, she was a tent leader. They won the trophy for the most points that year, and this is how she did it.

The guides were sent off on a small hike with their tent group. They had to find a safe place, set up a fire, cook sausages, and heat the beans up.

All the groups, except Vicky's of course, stayed close to the main camp.

Most groups couldn't get their fires started and called back for help. Vicky's group had walked a bit too far to call for help.

Instead, they ate the cold beans and tried to eat the sausages raw, but they were too disgusting.

Vicky's group got a lot of points for using their initiative, despite nearly giving themselves food poisoning.

It was definitely a different era back then, with a group of twelve-year-olds being allowed to wander over farmland, make a fire and cook for themselves.

I don't think it would be allowed now. Perhaps Vicky only half listened, or the Guide leaders didn't expect her to wander as far as she did. Who knows? But it was typical of her.

She was an early riser while camping and loved to go on walks in the woods. Each morning her tent group would go and collect wood for the open fire.

It was a way to stop them from getting in trouble for playing in the woods. A fire was kept lit all day and was used for cooking and boiling water.

The leader thought Vicky was showing good survival skills and gave her tent more points.

One evening the guides had been banned from having their tuck box of sweets from home. The tuck boxes were kept in the mess tent. Vicky was not happy, because she missed her sweets.

She asked two of her tent crew to distract the leader while she and another guide crawled in under the back of the tent to steal four tuck boxes, which she managed to do.

That night her tent group decided to have a midnight feast and rounded up the other guides quietly. Of course, they got caught and were sent back to their tents.

The next morning, Vicky was asked how she had got the sweet boxes.

She explained they all worked as a team, which actually impressed the leaders. Because they shared their sweets when the others didn't have any, they gave them more points.

This camping trip ended up being one of the highlights of her childhood.

My timelines are a bit mixed up here, because that's how memories work.

I was actually eleven when I first went camping with Agnes, and twelve during this trip, even though I have written it in my age ten chapter.

Childhood just blends together sometimes. I tried my best.

Once home, it wasn't long before Vicky was also allowed to go horse riding.

Her friend Denise went too. Denise's other friend had stopped going, so her mum asked Vicky's mum if Vicky wanted to have lessons with her.

At school, the girls had been talking about it, but Vicky thought her parents wouldn't let her go. They hatched a plan. Denise said, "Your mum won't say no to my mum, so I'll get her to phone yours."

When Ann asked Vicky, she jumped at the chance because she'd always wanted a horse for her birthday.

Denise told Vicky that if they helped clean out the stables on Sundays, they could get free rides.

Vicky started off having a few lessons in a ring and took to it well. Later, she started to join Denise on hacks, but her reins were still attached to the teacher.

As Vicky got her confidence up, the training reins were removed, and Vicky was in sole charge of her horse. It was all fun and games.

First, she was given a horse that just refused to move, so she had to get off and change to another.

But the next one decided to shake while Vicky was still on top. It was about to roll over, so she jumped off just in time.

Denise had been doing slow hacks and now wanted to do fast hacks where they cantered. Vicky was unsure, so she decided to ride a Shetland pony, thinking they ran slower.

Vicky didn't realise she was riding a lead horse, one that always wanted to be up front.

At first, she was given a whip, not to use but to hold it where the horse could see it, as this normally calmed it down.

On this particular day, the Shetland kept biting the backsides of the horses in front and suffered the odd kick in return. This made Vicky more nervous.

In an open field, the group decided a good canter was needed.

The Shetland was not happy he wasn't out in front, so he decided to make his own way across the field in a completely different direction.

He was heading for a large hedge, with a stream behind it. All Vicky could do was hold on tight, bouncing and bewildered.

She could hear hooves in the distance chasing after her, but this only made matters worse. The Shetland was determined to stay out in front.

Vicky and her horse were completely out of control. "Pull up, pull up, reins to right, reins to right!" She heard someone call from behind her.

Luckily, she did this at the last minute, narrowly missing being thrown into a muddy stream.

On a different day, it had been raining. Vicky was wearing a Johnny coat, as they were called back then. It was a clear, see-through plastic coat, and when she walked, the coat rattled.

A different horse either thought it was food or it was frightened of the noise. It started to follow Vicky and wouldn't leave her alone.

Vicky began to run around in circles. She decided to run between two parked cars, but for some reason, the horse was determined to get to Vicky.

The pony reared up and tried to climb the car bonnet.

From the tack room came a shout, "Take your jacket off and throw it at the horse!" Vicky obeyed very quickly. The pony stepped back, sniffed the jacket, and walked back to its stable.

Vicky decided to stop riding shortly after that. She'd developed a fear of horses unless there was a fence between them.

When she was riding, she was allowed to come on Sundays to groom the horses and muck out the stables.

Towards the end of the day, Denise asked about the free rides.

They were told that when they were finished, they could swap a few horses around. Some from the field and some back to the field, which was about a 15-minute trot.

Vicky and Denise had to ride them bareback.

If you haven't done it before, it can be painful. Their spine is wide and hard where you sit, and trotting means your pelvic area is being hit hard repeatedly.

Vicky ended up going to the doctors because she was unable to pee and was extremely bruised.

Her periods started around this point too, at ten or eleven years old. She never got back on a horse after that. I wonder why.

Camping came around quite quickly, even though it was toward the end of the summer. Nothing really happened, just the normal things, but the journey home was something different.

Gwen found one of Vicky's softballs that she had bought with her own holiday money. Gwen decided to throw it across to Agnes, Agnes threw it back while Vicky tried to retrieve it.

Agnes found it funny and opened the window just as Gwen threw it back, and yes, you guessed it, it went straight out of the car window.

Vicky started shouting at her sisters. John stopped the car, realised what had happened and yes, out of the car Vicky came. Guess who got the smacks.

Twenty-Five: Flooding School

It was Vicky's final year at primary school.

She hated playtimes. Most of the time, she entertained herself. She liked to do a lot of handstands up against the school walls, often flashing her knickers.

Vicky also liked to run around a brick pillar to see how dizzy she could get. Once she became bored, trouble usually found Vicky.

It was a chilly day, nobody wanted to play, and Vicky had nothing to do. She decided to line up and wait to go back inside. Being first in the line meant she could lean up against the latched door.

She found that if she pushed it with her back, the door would make an interesting click and spring back.

Vicky tried and tried again, trying to get it to double-click, then triple-click, and so on until a very cross head teacher came out of her office to see what all the noise was about.

"What on earth are you doing? I hope you do not do that to your doors at home," said the teacher in a stern voice. "No, Miss Loopy," Vicky said, holding back her fear.

"Maybe I should ring your parents to double-check. Where is your respect for school property?" Alarm bells started to ring in Vicky's head. "Oh no, I'll be beaten black and blue," she thought to herself.

It wasn't for the fact that she was being naughty but for the attention it would bring to the family, and the embarrassment it would bring to her father.

She had never been so scared as she was in that minute.

Vicky became angry.

She felt people just didn't give her a break, always telling her off, so now she needed to get her own back on Miss Loopy for threatening to call her parents, although she never did.

Vicky thought, "If I give Miss Loopy something else to worry about, she may just forget what I was doing earlier.

It must be something big." She had to think of something, so she started to hatch a plan.

The next day, Vicky kept on making excuses to go to the toilet. It was a place she could think without distractions. It wasn't until PE that she found her opportunity.

PE was held in the upper school hall. They had the mats out, and Vicky was trying to perfect her forward rolls.

Suddenly, her nose began to run, and she wiped it across her hand. As she looked down, there was blood across her knuckle.

She ran to her teacher to let him know she had a nosebleed. Mr Clarkson said, "It's OK, your nose isn't bleeding, but you might want to wash your face."

Vicky went off to the sinks. If you remember, they were in an alcove. Six sinks on each wall next to everybody's PE kit hanging on pegs.

Vicky looked into the mirror, horrified at what she saw. A huge, sticky, slimy red-green bogey stuck to the bridge of her nose. No wonder her classmates were staring.

How embarrassing. There was no way she could face her classmates now. What a nightmare.

Vicky noticed a bright red fire alarm on a white-washed wall and thought about setting it off. She also saw the door to the main playground, which meant a way home.

Nobody was around who would notice. Vicky remembered her previous plan; what could she do?

To begin with, she started to mess with all the PE kits of all the other classes hanging on the pegs.

She swapped out T-shirts, then shorts, then swapped out the odd plimsoll. Now everybody's PE kit was mixed up.

It didn't feel like enough, but now she was regretting what she had done. She couldn't fix it; she couldn't remember whose clothing she had mixed up.

Vicky went and turned the tap on to wash her hands and face, then dried them with blue paper towels. She looked at the paper towel crumpled in her hand and decided to plug the sink next to her.

Vicky wondered if this paper towel would be strong enough to actually hold water.

She turned the tap fully on, without realising the first sink was already overflowing. She had forgotten to turn it off while daydreaming.

Panicking, she grabbed a handful of paper towels and tried to mop it up. It wasn't working, all she ended up with was a soggy mess of wet paper towels.

She realised she was in a heap of trouble now. No matter what she did, she was going to be caught in style. Big time.

Vicky tried to remove the soggy tissues from the plug holes.

It wasn't going to budge. It just broke into pieces. With the tap turned off and the sink still dripping water on the floor, she began to pick up all the paper towels off the floor.

Soggy and dripping, she went to put them in the bin but realised they were too soggy for that. She decided to push them into all ten plug holes, hoping they would go down if she tore them up.

Vicky was stressed. Maybe she could blame it on someone else and tell the teacher she had found it like that and had tried to sort it out. That was why she was wet. Yes, that would work.

Vicky quickly stuffed all ten plugs with the soggy blue paper and turned on all ten sinks.

She waited until they all started to overflow before running back to her teacher to tell him what she had found and tried to stop it.

At home time, she saw her friendly caretaker cleaning all the mess up. It must have taken hours of cleaning.

Vicky felt a rock in her stomach. She felt so bad. If only Miss Loopy had to clean it up. Vicky could have smiled at that.

Now her friend was cleaning up her mess. She felt terrible and learned something that day.

She felt worse when the teacher gave her a *well-done*, excellent work star for her chart, for trying to clean it up and reporting it.

Twenty-Six: A Petition

Vicky began to show talent in sport, acting and maths. She was also starting to mature. Her breasts started to develop, and she'd started her periods.

Her last teacher at primary school was male. He liked Vicky because of her sporting ability. He was the one who took her when she ran for Shepway, the district team.

She was the fastest runner in the whole school and could even outrun John.

In some lessons, the teacher took the boys into the staff room to watch football on television and left the girls to read books. Vicky thought that was unfair.

When it came to PE, boys and girls were still getting changed together in the classrooms. They also had a male teacher watching over them.

Vicky started a petition and took it to the headmistress with Nina, of all people.

They wanted somewhere separate to change from the boys because girls were starting to wear bras and, for Vicky, because she had started her period.

Miss Loopy was really impressed with Vicky and gave her a star for the board. She believed the girls had gone about it in the right manner.

From then on, the girls could use the toilets for changing. Vicky had made this happen.

This is really the end of Vicky's primary school years. But one person needs another chapter all to herself.

Nanny Clara, Ann's mother.

She was the one Vicky loved most in the whole wide world. Probably because her nan could relate to Vicky's hardship, and vice versa.

Twenty-Seven: Nanny Clara

As I said before, Nanny Clara had had a really hard life. She was adopted, and her only half-sister was murdered.

Clara married a man who gambled. She gave away two of her children because she couldn't afford to keep them.

She loved all her children.

She kept photos of the ones who had been adopted in her handbag, and on a few occasions, normally when Vicky stayed the night, Vicky would catch her nan crying while looking at them.

She hadn't given up her children easily.

Although she loved her children, she didn't have much time for them.

Back in her day, clothes were washed by hand, which took up a lot of her time. She also went out to work as a chambermaid, cleaning and changing bedsheets at a hotel.

She loved to read the Bible and had a cross above her bed. When Vicky knew her, she lived in a three-storey townhouse.

It also had a basement with three rooms, which she kept locked up because the floorboards were rotten.

The railway line was across the road, and you could watch the Orient Express go past on its way to the pier. Her house was on its way to its final destination.

As you entered Nanny Clara's house, there was a thin hallway. To the left was a very damp bedroom, and next to it was a room with a sink and a mangle, her washroom.

There was a back door to the garden that was hard to open, and a small toilet under the staircase. The toilet leaned to the left and the floorboards were rotten.

Up the first flight of stairs was the kitchen and sitting room, and another flight took you to the two bedrooms. At the top, there wasn't a bathroom.

The house was old and very run-down. Vicky wasn't sure if it was just the era or that both sets of grandparents were simply poor.

Nanny Clara had sixteen grandchildren, but Vicky always felt she had time for her. Vicky didn't visit very often, usually only when Ann took her.

Nanny Clara probably gave more time to Vicky than she ever gave Ann. If Vicky was off sick from school, she went and spent the day with her nan.

Vicky never wanted to go home, so her nanny always tried to see if she could stay, and most of the time it worked.

There were times when John came to pick Vicky up, and he was quite curt with her.

Nanny Clara would say things like, "Why do you speak to her like that?" or, "She has a name. She's a little girl, have you forgotten?"

She took no nonsense from John and often put him in his place.

In front of him, she once said to Vicky, "If he ever speaks to you like that again or is too mean, just leave home and come live with me. You shouldn't have to put up with that."

Vicky found her nan to be very outspoken and cheeky.

If Vicky felt unwell, Nanny Clara would get Vicky to pretend she was ill, more than she was. Clara would say to John, "Oh, she's too ill to move, let her stay with me, I can look after her."

As soon as John left, Vicky got up and the biscuits came out. Nanny Clara loved to spoil her.

Her nan took her strawberry picking and showed her how to sneakily eat strawberries before buying them.

She would say, "Quick Vicky, this is a big, plump one! Eat it quick, crouch down so nobody can see."

She also took Vicky to the food shops and did the same with the fresh veg aisle. Nanny Clara's motto was, 'Don't buy it if you don't like it. Always try it first.

If Vicky told her off, her nan would push her false teeth out and wiggle them, which Vicky found funny.

Nanny Clara would tell stories that fascinated Vicky.

She told her bits and pieces about the war; she wished she had asked more questions about it. She told her about the ration book and hearing planes go overhead.

She was a very interesting character to be around.

Nanny Clara cleaned hotel rooms, and she always brought home toiletries. Vicky saw her nan in action once.

Whether it was because she was poor or a leftover habit from rationing days, if she saw an opportunity, she took it.

One night Vicky stayed over. She slept in bed with her nan while her grandad slept in the other room. Vicky saw the cross of Jesus on the wall and asked why she believed in God.

Clara said, "He came to my door and spoke to me." It had a long story that went with it.

Vicky asked, "Nanny, if you die, will you come back and tell me? Then I'll know to be religious too." Clara laughed and said, "Only if God lets me, but I'm sure he will."

On the way back from the shops one day, a boy on a skateboard was beating his dog because it wouldn't run and pull him along.

Vicky's nan said, "Shall we follow him home? I think his parents should know how he's treating his dog." She made it into a little game so the boy wouldn't notice them following.

As soon as the boy was home, Nanny Clara was banging on the door. The parents were very apologetic and told their son off in front of Vicky and her nan.

Nanny Clara found two stray cats. They were tiny, underweight little things. She picked them up and took them home. She didn't realise one of them was pregnant.

She ended up keeping all five kittens too. She had them all neutered and looked after them properly.

The only problem was that she played roughly with them, so they would bite anybody when they got bored.

She kept the litter tray by the front door, so anyone entering her house was met with the smell of cat urine.

Nanny Clara was always invited to Vicky's birthday parties. She would sing and dance, and mess about with her false teeth. Vicky's friends loved her too.

Vicky had birthday parties up to the age of ten. Her mum always made her birthday cake in the shape of whatever she wanted. Butterflies, cats, a house, a caterpillar, even a chocolate mess.

Vicky would invite around ten friends, and the entertainment was always party games and Nanny Clara being cheeky.

Then, as she got older, it became more of a disco for her birthday parties. Ann did this for all her children, and Vicky was always grateful.

John never attended. By the time he got home from work, the party atmosphere disappeared.

That was his party trick for Vicky.

Twenty-Eight: Stranger Danger

You may be wondering whether it was safe for kids under twelve to play on the streets back in the 70s and 80s.

Well, Vicky survived. There were fewer cars, for starters, and a lot less people. Back then, kids were taught to be wary of strangers.

Vicky's primary school sometimes had lock-ins because someone was behaving strangely outside.

The children were told of certain cars that had been hanging around the school gates and their drivers acting oddly.

The kids were told that if anyone approached them, they must never get into the car, even if the person said they knew their family. They were taught stranger danger.

Two bad stranger experiences happened to Vicky.

The first one was when she was around eight.

She was on her way to a pond. It was an exceptionally large pond that took a good half hour to walk around. There were lots of trees and shrubs around it and plenty of quiet fishing spots.

Vicky had been on school trips for pond dipping there. It was also very deep, so you had to be careful you didn't fall in.

Three of Agnes's friends had been to the pond earlier and left because a man in a car had been following them.

They left because they were scared. On their way home, they bumped into Vicky and her friends heading to where they had come from. They smiled but didn't speak.

As usual, Vicky and her friends went to the pond with their nets, because they wanted to find and catch things.

Vicky knew to stay in the open bits, the areas with fewer trees so they could still see the road.

A red car had parked, and a man in his twenties to thirties was leaning on it with his back to the driver's door.

Vicky noticed him watching them and told her friends. They all assumed he was waiting for his family.

It was only when Ann turned up at the pond, a walk that took her about twenty minutes, that Vicky found out this man was someone to fear.

Agnes's friends had turned up at Ann's door to warn her that Vicky was heading the same way they had been when a man followed them.

He had approached one of the girls when she was just out of sight of her friends. Her friend came back just in time.

She had been trying a different spot to net some newts. She found one and went back to show her friend.

This guy was holding her friend's arm and talking to her. They all got a bit scared, said they were late home, and ran off.

He followed them until he saw Vicky and her friends. The man turned back, followed Vicky and her friends to the pond, and then watched them from the road.

Vicky saw the man still staring and pointed him out to her mum. Ann gathered up Vicky and all her friends, told them to link arms and stay close.

Ann walked them all safely home. Ann told their parents what had happened. Vicky was told to never go to that place again. She never did.

Another time, when Vicky was in her final year of primary school, she liked to go over to the hills and climb. It was good fun sliding down long grass, you went really fast.

To get there, you had to climb over a stile, into a wheat field and follow a track into a small wood. You'd come out into a clearing at the bottom of the hill.

Now, in this clearing was a man whose trousers were undone, and he was fiddling with himself in broad daylight, right in full view of the path.

Vicky and her friends stopped in their tracks; they couldn't believe what they were seeing. They ended up taking the long way round him and just carried on with their day.

Why Vicky and her friends didn't get out of there straight away, I will never understand.

Vicky's childhood had come to an end. She was now entering her teenage years.

Sneak Peek

The Long Road to Finding Me: The Teen Years

Here's a short glimpse of Vicky's teenage years.

By the time Vicky reached secondary school, behaving herself was no longer an option. It wasn't a choice; it was a survival. And survival, for her, meant mischief.

Vicky's history teacher was a shy French woman who could barely control the class. She had a habit of hiding in her little walk-in cupboard when things got too much.

She would go inside with her flask, shut the door, and hope for a moment of peace, until her nerves calmed.

One day, the moment her back was turned, Vicky saw her chance. She crept up, swung the cupboard door shut, and locked it.

The class erupted into laughter. A few children patted her on the back, thrilled someone had finally done what everyone else was thinking. Then they all went quiet.

A tiny voice drifted through the door, shaky and confused, complete with a French accent.

"Hello? Is anyone there? I think the door is stuck. Please… I need help."

For a moment, Vicky felt powerful.
Then guilt set in, not the "oops, accident" kind, but the "I shouldn't have done that" kind.

She unlocked the door and said gently,
"It was stuck, Miss. You should get that looked at."

The class sniggered behind her.

Vicky waved a warning.

Don't you dare tell.

Oh, there is so much more to come.

About the Author

Lily Lane is the author of The Long Road to Finding Me. She is dyslexic, and this book is written the way she reads, in short, spaced sentences that allow the story to flow without overwhelming the reader.

This memoir is drawn from lived experience and told with honesty, care, and reflection.

You can follow Lily's writing at:

lilylaneauthor.substack.com

Printed in Dunstable, United Kingdom